Teaching and Learning About
MULTICULTURAL
LITERATURE
Students Reading Outside Their Culture
in a Middle School Classroom

JANICE HARTWICK DRESSEL
Central Michigan University
Mount Pleasant, Michigan, USA

INTERNATIONAL
Reading Association
800 Barksdale Road, PO Box 8139
Newark, Delaware 19714-8139, USA
www.reading.org

Director of Publications   Joan M. Irwin
Editorial Director, Books and Special Projects   Matthew W. Baker
Production Editor   Shannon Benner
Permissions Editor   Janet S. Parrack
Acquisitions and Communications Coordinator   Corinne M. Mooney
Associate Editor, Books and Special Projects   Sara J. Murphy
Assistant Editor   Charlene M. Nichols
Administrative Assistant   Michele Jester
Senior Editorial Assistant   Tyanna L. Collins
Production Department Manager   Iona Sauscermen
Supervisor, Electronic Publishing   Anette Schütz
Senior Electronic Publishing Specialist   Cheryl J. Strum
Electronic Publishing Specialist   R. Lynn Harrison
Proofreader   Elizabeth C. Hunt

Project Editors   Janet S. Parrack, Matthew W. Baker, and Shannon Benner

Cover   Design, Linda Steere; Image, Creatas

Library of Congress Cataloging-in-Publication Data
Dressel, Janice Hartwick.
    Teaching and learning about multicultural literature : students reading outside their culture in a middle school classroom / Janice Hartwick Dressel.
        p.   cm.
Includes bibliographical references and index.
    ISBN 0-87207-457-9 (alk. paper)
1. Multicultural education.   2. Language arts (Middle school).   I. Title.
    LC1099.D74 2003
    370.117—dc21
                                                                                        2002015188

CONTENTS

ACKNOWLEDGMENTS

There are always many debts in an undertaking like this. They can seldom be repaid but at least they can be acknowledged.

This project could never have been completed without the personal dedication of the teacher who designed the unit and taught the students, provided me with students' writing, kept a journal during the teaching of the unit, and permitted me to publish whatever conclusions emerged after analyzing the materials. To protect the identity of the students she taught, the teacher must remain anonymous. Because of this, she will never receive public credit for her effort or her courage. However, the children and teachers who benefit from the findings of this study will be forever indebted to her.

Next, I owe a debt of gratitude to my husband, Dave, for his understanding and support through the past several years. His conviction that I would complete this project carried me through innumerable crises. I thank him especially for his patient listening but also for feeding me when I didn't have time to eat, for completing the tasks I often had to put aside, and for the myriad of other things he did but thought I didn't notice.

Special thanks go to Dr. Felix Famoye and Dr. Carl Lee, both professors of statistics and consulting statisticians at Central Michigan University. They patiently gave of their time and expertise to help me design the study and analyze the results.

Denise Jacobs gave selflessly of her time and energy to understand nondominant cultures and the goals of this study. Without her commitment and dedication to the honest evaluation of the students' papers, none of this would have come into being.

The many students I have taught over the years deserve special mention. Their dedication to understanding the lives of others has provided constant encouragement. Thanks, too, to those students who have worked with me this fall on revision—both theirs and mine.

Matt Baker of the International Reading Association deserves special thanks for the extra effort he expended to help bring this book to completion.

Central Michigan University provided a sabbatical leave to help me complete this project and also provided funds for the second independent rater.

The final debt is to my family and friends who continue to love and support me in spite of the time and energy that work on this project has involved, especially my parents, Helen and Ernie Hartwick. The following people also deserve special mention:

Mark and Sue and Stacie
Sherri and Mark
Nancy Kopka, Lois Simon, and Beth Sipple Janick
People of Martin Luther Chapel

—*JHD*

[Multicultural literature] opens an ethnic group's heart to the reading public.... The voice coming from the heart, once heard, will change hearts. For the author's voice to be heard, the silent words on the pages need to be read and responded to by the reader. (Cai, 1992, p. 26)

C ai makes it sound so easy. But is it that easy for readers to change? How can we, as teachers, help readers to hear? How do we help them to respond? How do we help them to see into the hearts of ethnic groups other than their own?

Literature has long been seen as a socializing agent, and more recently multicultural literature has been promoted as "a powerful tool to help students develop an understanding and respect for individuals of all cultures while at the same time gaining an appreciation of their own cultural and literary heritage" (Young, Campbell, & Oda, 1995, p. 377). Many educators believe that "multicultural literature can be a powerful vehicle for accomplishing [the] task" of changing the world "by making it a more equitable one" (Bishop, 1992, p. 51). Children's literature textbooks promote multicultural literature, and almost any professional language arts or literacy journal contains articles that claim that incorporating multicultural literature into the curriculum is an easy and effective way of facilitating cultural awareness and positive understanding (see Macphee, 1997; Walker-Dalhouse, 1992). Although the professional literature is full of discussion about using multicultural literature in the classroom, little systematic study has been dedicated to the examination of classroom practice and the outcomes in achieving such literacy. In a theoretical and historical overview of 20th-century reader-response theorists, Cox (1992) writes that "the missing voice in this dialogue is, of course, that of real readers engaged with real texts in real contexts" (p. 20). Although some efforts are being made to fill this void (Cruz, Jordan, Melendez, Ostrowski, & Purves, 1997; Rogers & Soter, 1997; Trimmer & Tilly, 1992), much remains to be done. Rudine Sims Bishop (1997), a preeminent leader in the field of multicultural literature, argues that rather than be satisfied with merely exposing readers to a variety of texts, we need to determine effective instructional strategies to confront the problems of the past:

> For readers who are members of dominant groups, the *assumption* has been that becoming acquainted with and finding their own connections to literature about people from nondominant groups would help them to value all peoples, accept differences as a natural aspect of human societies, and even celebrate cultural pluralism as a desirable feature of the world in which they live. (pp. vii–viii) [italics added]

Recently, the professional debate has focused on "the need for multicultural literature and (paradoxically) the limitations of reader-response theories (as they are currently constituted) to speak to the actual responses of diverse readers" (Rogers & Soter, 1997, p. 1). Treating literature as if it is an aesthetic creation separate from the real world and its political contexts is becoming increasingly suspect. As more multicultural books become available, it becomes increasingly important to know what children are learning about cultures from the books they read. Does multicultural literature lead dominant-culture readers to value people of other cultures? Does it encourage them to accept and value differences and to embrace cultural pluralism? And how does reader response fit into the puzzle?

If readers are at least as important as texts in the meaning that emerges when the two come together, what happens when white readers read stories about nonwhite characters? Perhaps merely exposing readers to multicultural texts isn't enough. Assuming that it is enough would mean that readers are relatively passive receptacles, which, of course, isn't true. Over the past few years, my university students, who are primarily white, have become more insistent that any meaning they make is acceptable because they bring unique experiences to the text. And that isn't true either. If our goal is to understand others and ourselves better through the appreciation of literature, we must recognize that both the reader and the text are important. Although there is no single interpretation of a text, a defensible reading needs to account for as many elements of the text as possible but, at the same time, must not assume that elements are present that are not (Rosenblatt, 1938/1976).

Social Responsibility and Reader Response

Not long ago, I read an article (Harris, 1994) that helped me to make sense of these disparate perspectives. "Maybe," Harris writes, "we expect too much of those who have been excluded; those who exclude must bear equal responsibility" (p. 11). As Harris infers, those people who have the power to change things bear much responsibility for making the world a more equitable one. At the present time, that means those who are white and currently benefit from systems designed to favor one group of people over another only because of color.

As I reflected on Harris's comments, it occurred to me that maybe claiming *any* meaning to be acceptable was just another example of the dominant culture using theory—in this case, the theory of reader response—to justify and solidify an existing power position. As Purves (1993) notes, "Readers are not naive…[they] bring a great deal to the text" (p. 349). Peggy McIntosh (1989) argues that whites receive unrecognized benefits just from being white. They have the unearned advantage and arbitrarily awarded power of being white. She further argues that whites are carefully taught not to recognize that being white *systemically* confers unearned power on their group not because of anything they have done but simply because they were born with white skin.

The dilemma for classroom teachers is profound. Teachers try to help students love literature, but at the same time they feel a responsibility to encourage students to understand better the literature and lives of people different from themselves. Often bound by a fairly traditional literature curriculum, teachers struggle with this task. Yet few have had the opportunity to reflect about culture in general, let alone about specific cultures and multicultural literature in particular. And most middle school students have little, if any, knowledge about the values, beliefs, social practices, or arts of cultures other than their own. In fact, most students are in the process of defining themselves within their own cultures, and cultures are by nature exclusionary. So, what is to be done?

The Purpose of This Book

The purpose of this book is to help teachers teach multicultural literature more effectively. By sharing what happened when 123 dominant-culture eighth graders read multicultural books, I hope to provoke your thinking about your own classroom. In doing so, I may challenge assumptions about teaching, learning, and cultures. My goal is to help teachers and students have a richer experience reading all literature, particularly multicultural literature and, by doing so, to begin to understand themselves and others better. Although the readers I talk about are primarily white, what I say in the following pages has much more to do with differences in power than it does with differences in color.

Because differences in power exist between and among peoples of all ages, genders, and ethnicities, I hope the findings I discuss will interest you as a teacher regardless of your students' backgrounds.

This book is the story one teacher's students told in their writing, although they often were unaware that they were telling it. A different story might have resulted from an analysis of students' oral discourse. Writing permits us to stand apart from our thinking and to consider what we are saying. Because it is separate from the judgment of the peer group, writing enables middle school students to express themselves in ways they cannot orally.

The Story and Its Tellers

> I feel like a failure...but I'm not sure what else I could have done.... I hope they really learned something. I will definitely teach this unit again, but I will have to change much of what I did. (Ann)

Ann (a pseudonym) taught eighth grade in a white, middle-class suburb of a large midwestern U.S. city. This was the first time she had taught a multicultural unit, and as you can tell, she did not feel successful. According to Cai (1997),

> From the perspective of social progress, multicultural literature is intended to inform people about other cultures, to liberate them from the bondage of stereotypes...to foster respect for one's own cultural heritage as well as others, and to promote cross-cultural understanding. (p. 210)

Given the assumptions that educators have long held about the impact multicultural literature has on dominant-culture readers, it seems reasonable to think that the novels Ann's students read would have challenged their perceptions of the world and caused them to change their way of understanding the world to accommodate the discrepancies. However, their understandings did not change. Why not?

In *Teaching and Learning About Multicultural Literature: Students Reading Outside Their Culture in a Middle School Classroom*, you will hear Ann's voice and you will hear the voices of her students. Although Ann consulted with me frequently as she prepared the multicultural literature unit discussed in the following pages, she designed and taught the unit as part of her normal yearly curriculum. She also kept a journal, documenting for me what she did in preparation for the unit, what she did during the teaching of it, and what she reflected on after it was finished. The students' voices emerge from the writing that they completed during the unit.

I am the researcher and narrator. As a professor at a midsized university in the midwestern United States, my areas of expertise are literature for children and young adults, particularly multicultural and international literature, and the teaching of writing in elementary and middle school. Although I now teach English education at the university level, my career began as a public school teacher. Because I live 600 miles from Ann and her students, I was not in the classroom with them. Like most teachers, Ann had set a number of goals for her students (see chapter 1). My role was to examine the written work that Ann's four classes of eighth graders completed during the unit and to determine if Ann and her students had met those goals.

What You Can Expect From This Book

This study is what statisticians call a descriptive study. The findings I discuss come from both quantitative and qualitative analyses. Throughout this book, I share the results of the statistical analysis and explain my interpretation of those analyses. I have tried to provide a clear description of the context to help you understand my interpretation. And, because all research is conducted and interpreted in the context of other research, I also share the findings of other researchers. In trying to understand what happened in Ann's room, I read articles, books, reports, and other work by many other researchers who explained what they had done and their findings. Because these findings helped me interpret my own research, I describe the relevant studies so you can decide whether you agree with my understanding of what occurred in Ann's classroom. For example, throughout this book, I present statistical results followed by examples of students' written work. This procedure is based on the recommendations of Martin (1980), who suggests that both the statistical information and the actual written responses need to be included to provide a complete picture of the results. Martin's research goal was to determine if reading literature written by black authors affected the attitudes of white readers. After analyzing the attitudes of 435 white, suburban, ninth-grade students before and after a four-month experience reading such literature, Martin found the quantitative results disappointing: The statistics did not show many of the changes that occurred in students' writing. Because students' written responses "revealed that clear, positive attitudinal changes emerged in a number of individual cases," Martin concluded that including "more subjective kinds of response such as written reactions" (p. 45) would have provided more complete results. I thought this was an important idea. As a result, I included written responses from Ann's students to provide concrete examples of the kinds of responses the statistics are measuring—not just to make this interesting reading but because Martin concluded that doing so provides two sides of the picture. Throughout the following pages, I talk about other researchers, too, sharing their findings and how those findings provide insight into what occurred in Ann's classroom.

The closer your situation approximates Ann's classroom, the more directly you can apply what you read here to your own teaching and students' learning. Even if there is great divergence between your situation and Ann's, many of the findings I discuss will resonate with your knowledge of teaching and learning. It is my hope that my conclusions about what happened in Ann's classroom will stimulate you to reflect on your classroom, your teaching, and your students' learning.

Throughout the chapters of this book, I share recommendations that emerged from analyzing the students' written work. To set the stage for those recommendations, chapter 1 briefly discusses several theoretical frameworks related to the teaching of literature and why the teaching of multicultural literature is creating controversy among educators in the United States and elsewhere. I introduce Ann and describe the school system, the students (pseudonyms have been used for the teacher and students), and the unit. Next, I identify the literature the students read and explain the unit assignments. Finally, I describe the Evaluation Instrument—how it was developed, how it was used to analyze students' work, and how the information was compiled.

In chapter 2, I describe what I found about students' affective and aesthetic responses to the books they read, the findings from other research, and suggestions that are based on the findings.

In chapter 3, I examine what students' writing revealed in relation to their learning about cultures and people different from themselves. I share insights from other researchers to set the findings of the study in a broader context. The findings from this study are rich with information and, taken in the context of what we can learn from other research, provide a firm foundation for suggestions about classroom activity.

In chapter 4, I reflect on what happened in Ann's classroom and explain why it happened. I describe forces that operated within and outside the classroom that affected the readers, and I take a close look at the role the teacher played in relation to what students learned when they read multicultural literature.

In chapter 5, I summarize the findings and offer concrete suggestions for what you can do in your own classroom to help students integrate personal response and social responsibility, which is no easy task.

In the appendixes, I provide samples of the primary student assignments: the Book Club Organizer, the Dialogue Journal, and the Pre-Unit and Post-Unit Surveys. I also include the Evaluation Instrument, so you can see what questions I asked of the students' writing, and the Rubric for Training Raters, which provides additional background about how the raters interpreted the questions.

This book is more than the story of one teacher and one classroom as they read multicultural literature together. It is the story of how the readers can enrich our approach to reading, response, and cultural understanding. It is my hope that the courage of this teacher, in sharing her story with its successes and its disappointments, will encourage you and your students to listen more effectively to "the silent words on the pages" (Cai, 1992, p. 26) of multicultural literature and to hear them with your hearts.

CHAPTER I

The Story Begins: The Theory, the Context, the Research

Teaching multicultural literature is a double responsibility—to the literature and to the group of people—the culture—that the literature claims to reflect. The teacher must know as much as possible about the culture in the novel and must address issues of culture, stereotypes, outsider versus insider perspective, cultural authenticity, and cultural differences so that respect for diversity is promoted rather than ethnocentricity and prejudice being reinforced. We must be aware of the power of literature to influence thinking and that many people believe everything they read. (Ann)

Ann takes teaching seriously, and her commitment to teaching, to the literature, and to the cultures it reflects is revealed in her words. This chapter touches on different theories relating to the teaching of literature and explains why the teaching of multicultural literature is creating controversy among educators in the United States and elsewhere. As you become acquainted with Ann and her stance in relation to theory, compare your thinking and practice with hers. Whether or not your situation is similar to Ann's, you will find the results interesting.

The Theory

The Focus on Texts

During the early years of the 20th century, many educators believed that if readers could decode the words on the page, the meaning of the text would be clear. They believed that meaning was in the text. Some educators still believe this. Another group of educators also believed that meaning resided in the text. These theorists ascribed to a school of thought referred to as Formalism or New Criticism. Their heavy focus on the inherent value of the text meant that they paid less attention to the reader or the context of the reading. Although this school of thinking was prominent from the 1920s until the 1960s, Rosenblatt (1938/1976) was writing about readers' responses as early as the 1930s. But it was not until the late 1960s, with educators' reactions to the rigid tenor of analytic, scientific thinking, that theories with a strong focus on the reader found a more receptive audience.

The Focus on Readers

The past 50 years have seen a shift in focus in the professional literature from the text to the reader and, often, the reader in a specific context. Bakhtin (1981), Bleich (1975), Britton (1970), Fish (1980), Harding (1962), Holland (1975), Iser (1974, 1978), and Rosenblatt (1938/1976, 1978, 1985), among others, have all developed theories of what occurs when readers respond to text. Although there are significant differences in their descriptions of what occurs, as well as the weight given to the reader, the text, and the context, all recognize a much more significant role for the reader than in the past.

The reader's purpose for reading influences the outcome of the reading event. Most of the reading children do in school is what Rosenblatt calls "efferent reading." In efferent reading, students are expected to analyze and evaluate what they read using preexisting criteria. Reading in this way means that readers become responsible for the accuracy of the text. Readers check the validity of the material read against the criteria. For example, they might look for flaws, question the text, or compare the text with other information that might challenge the content. According to Rosenblatt (1985), "the predominantly efferent reader focuses attention on public meaning, abstracting what is to be retained after the reading—to be recalled, paraphrased, acted on, analyzed" (p. 101).

However, Rosenblatt (1938/1976) and other prominent theorists such as Applebee (1978), Britton (1970), and Langer (1994) argue that efferent reading is not appropriate for literary texts. Although each theorist describes what happens in the reading event differently, all acknowledge that the way in which a reader approaches a text—the stance the reader takes—will influence the reader's role in the reading event. To read literature effectively, the reader needs to participate in a personal experience created when the individual reader uses the words on the page to create what Rosenblatt (1978) refers to as a "unique poem." Calling this aesthetic reading, Rosenblatt (1985) explains that "the reader's selective attention is focused primarily on what is being personally lived through, cognitively and affectively, *during* the reading event" (pp. 101–102). This transaction between the reader and the text results in a new and unique poem. Lee Galda (1992) says, "readers meet texts and, together, they create stories" (p. 127).

Ann's students approached reading from both stances during the multi-cultural unit. For example, Tom's writing indicated that he approached reading from an efferent stance. When he wrote about *Journey of the Sparrows* (Buss 1991), he provided an account of what he read rather than participating in the experience as it happened:

> The character I selected was Maria. Maria is a 15 year old girl who cam to America from El Salvador...a lot has happened. Maria has been fired from her job and was almost shipped back to El Salvador. Julia has had her baby. Maria has found work at the church....

(Note: Throughout the book, student writing samples are produced verbatim.)

Aaron, on the other hand, reflects an aesthetic stance in his writing about *Shadow of the Dragon* (Garland, 1993). Using the words on the page, Aaron re-created a new world, suspending disbelief and tacitly accepting the rules within that world until the story was over. To make sense of the story, he analyzed, synthesized, and evaluated, but always within his understanding of the parameters established by the author:

> My cousin Sang Le is coming to America from Hong-Kong where he was in a re-education camp and a refugee camp. I had to take him to his classes the first day he was at school and he is in ESL so that is where he spends his days. Calvin (a friend) and I are working on a science project now and I think it will turnout preety cool if we ever finish. (I forgot to buy the battery pack!)

Although it was possible for students to adopt either stance while completing Ann's assignments, as Tom and Aaron indicate in their Dialogue Journals, students usually assumed particular stances when completing the Book Club Organizer (see Appendix A) or the Dialogue Journal (see Appendix B). Because the Book Club Organizer asked students to outline the plot, describe the setting, identify the theme, and describe any differences between their world and the world of the text, students' writing usually reflected an efferent stance. And because the Dialogue Journal asked each student to assume the persona of a character and write to a peer outside the story world, most responded as if they were personally living through the events in the story, thus reflecting more of an aesthetic stance.

Today, the focus has shifted from the text to the reader. Although advocates of what is frequently called the reader response theory vary in their adherence to Rosenblatt's transactional theory, all would agree that some interaction between reader and text is indispensable. Some even argue, as my students have learned, that the reader is all-important, and any meaning the reader makes is acceptable. Rosenblatt (1938/1976) contends, however, that aesthetic reading, while indispensable, is only the beginning. As early as 1938 she wrote,

> The fact that the personal contribution of the reader is an essential element in any vital reading of literature justifies the demand that the teacher create a setting that makes it possible for the student to have a spontaneous response to literature. But...this represents only the first step, absolutely essential though that first step is. Once the student has responded freely, a process of growth can be initiated. He needs to learn to handle with intelligence and discrimination the personal factors that enter into his reaction to books. Through a critical scrutiny of his response to literary works, he can come to understand his personal attitudes and gain the perspective needed for a fuller and sounder response to literature. (p. 108)

The contemporary focus on individual response as an end in itself rather than the "starting point for criticism" (Rosenblatt, 1985, p. 103) has resulted in a bastardization of Rosenblatt's theory and, in many cases, a return to the destructive reader versus text controversy. The current focus on multicultural education has further complicated the issue for teachers of English and the language arts.

The Challenges of Multicultural Literature

According to Purves (1993),

> At this moment in the history of the world, a cultural view of literature is what will sustain it in the schools, more so than the moral view, or the universalistic view, or the aesthetic view.... Any other view, such as a textual view or a reader response view, will only serve to perpetuate implicitly what the Western canon perpetuates explicitly. (p. 358)

As previously noted, treating literature as if it exists as an aesthetic creation separate from the real world is becoming increasingly suspect. According to Cai (1997), from the perspective of social progress, multicultural literature is intended to inform people about other cultures, to liberate them from the bondage of stereotypes to foster respect for one's own cultural heritage as well as others, and to promote cross-cultural understanding. (p. 210)

This highlights the need to recognize Rosenblatt's insistence that readers' spontaneous response to literature is essential, but not enough. Especially when readers are reading outside their own cultures, it is imperative that teachers help them go beyond their spontaneous responses. Readers need to examine the personal factors that are part of their responses in order to gain fuller perspectives of cultures different from their own—a perspective that is more consistent with the culture reflected in the literature being read. Purves (1993) writes,

> When one considers only the text or the reader as many contemporary pedagogies do, one is tacitly assuming a monocultural view, a view that denies the roots of a literary work and the intellectual and cultural struggle that has produced it. It is to assume a "universalism" that is, as Said (1993) has so cogently pointed out, a form of imperialism. The cultural view of literature and literature teaching, a view that sees literary works in their historical and cultural context rather than as disembodied texts, is the only moral basis upon which we can build a Literature program. (p. 358)

Jordan and Purves (1993) describe *culture* as "a combination of (a) a set of intellectual beliefs and social practices of a self-defined group of people, and (b) the arts that embody those beliefs" (p. 1). They note that cultures are, by definition, exclusionary and that people of one culture see people of other cultures as "outside, above, or beneath them" (p. 1). Because literature is written by writers situated within specific cultures, it is both an aesthetic object and a cultural artifact. Jordan and Purves assert that multicultural texts should be read in the spirit of the culture, not simply for the "'significance' of the text, that which we, distant from that culture, make of it" (p. 2). Different people define multicultural literature differently depending on their purposes. Sometimes, *multicultural literature* refers to literature by and about people outside the dominant culture within the United States, but sometimes people use the term to refer to literature by and about any people who are not European American, which is how Ann used the term.

Studying high schools in nine countries, Purves, Foshay, and Hansson (1973) found clear cultural differences in the way students respond to literature, and discovered that those differences reflect the teaching emphases to which students are exposed. These teaching emphases reflect the critical traditions of particular countries. In the United States, such conditioning is already pronounced by the end of junior high. But in 1990, typical U.S. high school classrooms still did not reflect the focus on the reader that was prominent in the professional literature (Applebee, 1990). The text was still accepted as primary. Teachers still taught as if the meaning resided in the printed story, and the reader's job was to distill that meaning. The impact of the reader in the interaction still was not recognized.

Ann found herself caught in this conflict between a focus on the text and a focus on the reader. Having recently completed a master's degree in secondary education, she had read the professional literature that called for increased participation of the reader and less focus on the text itself. However, her entire undergraduate education had involved text analysis. She enjoyed it, felt she was good at it, and wanted to teach it. The conflict resulted in an intense internal struggle.

Ann recognized that both personal response to literature and learning about other cultures were necessary, but given her background, she found it difficult to balance the two. She didn't feel that validating readers' personal contributions was enough, especially because she had discovered that previous experiences in elementary and middle school had taught many of her students that responding personally was all they were expected to do. Ann believed that they needed to go beyond personal response—to participate in critical thinking about the text and about their own response to it. However, it is important to recognize that except perhaps for the question on one assignment that asked, "How does [the world your characters live in] compare and/or contrast with the world you live in?" Ann's written assignments did not intentionally involve her students in scrutinizing the way their own attitudes influenced their responses to the stories they read. Because they didn't come to understand how their own personal attitudes influenced their reading, students appeared unable to attain the perspective Rosenblatt (1978) argues is necessary for "a fuller and sounder response to literature" (p. 108). This ultimately led to Ann's disappointment with the unit, and the internal struggle that emerged in the pages of her journal. She was aware of the strong reader response movement in the United States and felt she needed to support readers' personal responses. She wanted to do that. In fact, Ann's primary goal for the unit was that students enjoy reading and understanding a novel. However, she also felt that she needed to take them beyond that initial response. Ann's interaction with her students had taught her that many were caught in the self-fulfilling prophecy that middle school was a place to mark time between elementary school and high school. Students didn't expect to think critically, and few knew how to respond when they were challenged intellectually. During other units, Ann accepted and validated students' responses but insisted that the class focus on the literature rather than themselves. She acknowledged that she was the interpretive authority in the classroom. But the multicultural unit was different; it was unlike any she had taught before. In this unit, Ann's goal was for students to like the books they read. To reach this goal, she gave students significant responsibility for interpretation. This unit was new territory for both the teacher and the students.

The Context

The Participants and the Setting

Ann, the classroom teacher in the study, had graduated from an Ivy League university with a degree in English and immediately enrolled in a one-year master's program in education. She student-taught in an upper-middle-class high school classroom and was hired, immediately after graduation, to teach in the middle school where this study took place. In Ann's second year of teaching, she was one of three teachers to win a districtwide award for outstanding teaching. Forty-five different teachers were nominated for the award by students, staff, parents, and community members. The following qualities about Ann were among those quoted in the school paper:

A parent: I was really impressed with how well she knew my son's abilities.

A student: She cares about us as people too. She encourages me to pursue things I really want to do. She always tells us to work hard.

A teacher: She individualizes the work so that each person has a chance to contribute and feel important. She feels strongly that students feel good about themselves by proving to themselves what they can accomplish. Students work hard in her class, and they feel successful.

The school was located in a suburb 10 miles from a major midwestern U.S. city. There were approximately 200 students in each grade, sixth through eighth, for a total of nearly 600 students. According to Ann, the student population was "[more than] 95% white, with a fairly middle-class SES [socioeconomic status], although there is a sizeable portion of lower SES families and students in the district." Although math class was tracked, other classes were not. Ann was a regular classroom teacher for English and taught 123 of the 200 eighth graders, of which 93% were white and U.S. citizens, 7% were nonwhite or non–U.S. citizens, 51% were female, and 49% were male. Ann also stated, "There is a very wide range of students within one class, from special education students who have difficulty writing a sentence to the likely candidates for valedictorian who breeze through the most difficult assignments." Although the average class size was 30 students, the actual breakdown for the four periods was 32, 27, 31, and 33 students. Classes met daily for 50 minutes.

The Teacher's Goals and Objectives

Knowing what she wanted her students to achieve and how she planned to help them achieve those goals was imperative for Ann. She wrote in her journal,

> Having clear and specific outcomes for a unit is the first essential step.... Without these outcomes, there is no focus and little sense of accomplishment at the end of the unit for the teacher or for the students. The outcomes create the frame for the unit, and all the thousands of decisions you must make fall into place much more easily with that frame.

Ann worked concomitantly with three sets of goals: the school district's outcomes for eighth-grade English, what she called her own "most basic goals" for herself and her students, and her outcomes for the multicultural literature unit. The summer prior to the study, Ann and the other three English teachers worked together to develop the following district outcomes for eighth-grade English:

- Students will be able to write for different audiences with a variety of purposes (formal essay, creative writing, research paper, journalism).
- Students will be able to read and interpret a variety of literature (historical fiction, science fiction, multicultural fiction, poetry, comedy) and literary terms (theme, mood, tone, point of view, conflict, foreshadowing, characterization, irony).
- Students will be able to demonstrate effective speaking skills in a variety of speaking situations (organization, nonverbal language, verbal techniques).
- Students will be able to demonstrate and apply techniques of effective listening (nonverbal cues, comprehension, reinforcement of speaker).

Based on these outcomes, Ann generated her basic goals for students:

- to think critically, especially understanding multiple viewpoints
- to use writing as a tool for self-understanding and expression
- to read, understand, and enjoy different types of literature
- to understand and identify elements of literature
- to understand the structure and purpose of a literary essay and be able to write one effectively
- to speak effectively with poise in front of a group
- to plan time responsibly by organizing a notebook, doing homework regularly, using work time well, and making decisions about how to handle the assignment load

Ann planned her teaching in four- to five-week units and designed each unit's outcomes to be consistent with the eighth-grade curriculum and her most basic goals. The multicultural literature unit was developed because she knew that her students needed more exposure to and experience with multicultural texts. The multicultural unit was the fifth of eight units taught this particular year from February 6 to March 17, the beginning of the third quarter.

Based on the eighth-grade outcomes, her own goals, and her knowledge of her students as readers and class members, Ann developed the following broad objectives for her students during the multicultural literature unit:

- to enjoy reading and understanding a novel
- to learn about the norms and values of cultures different from their own
- to understand themselves, their cultural values, and their cultural norms more clearly

Anticipating Difficulties

Ann intentionally taught the multicultural literature unit during the third quarter of the school year to ensure that students had the background they needed to support success. By this time of year, they would have read a selection of short stories and two novels; written a research paper, a book about themselves, a fable, and a literary essay; made four class presentations (including a skit, information report, personal anecdote, and character analysis); and written weekly in a student-to-teacher personal journal, or thinkbook, to which Ann would respond. The students would have defined and discussed plot, character, mood, setting, tone, point of view, theme, conflict, foreshadowing, flashback, and turning point.

However, Ann knew that most students in her four classes were not avid readers and had little experience with multicultural literature. Although she knew they had participated at different grade levels in various units about 17th-century Native Americans, and occasionally had read stories written by or about people of color, she also knew that few had ever grappled with the issues surrounding culture and cultural status in today's world reflected in multicultural literature.

As good teachers do, Ann tried to anticipate the difficulties her students would face in working to achieve the goals of the multicultural literature unit. Because of their limited experience with multicultural texts, she anticipated that they would exhibit the following behaviors as they read about characters from different cultures:

- Make quick generalizations about the cultural group in the novel and apply them to all members of that culture.
- Accept the presentation of the cultural group without questioning the novel or the author.
- Judge the characters based on the standards of the dominant culture (western-European American) standards.
- Ignore or fail to see the impact that being members of a nondominant culture has on the lives of the characters.
- See the characters as "victims" rather than as people with a whole range of human experience.
- Require more teacher guidance and assistance than could be provided during a book club unit.

From past experience with units designed around a novel, Ann knew that some students would not keep up with the reading; some of the students would find their books a bit boring, especially in the beginning; and the class would have problems with small-group functioning. And she knew from reading Donelson and Nilson (1989) "that young teens have short attention spans. A variety of activities should be organized so that participants can remain active as long as they want and then go on to something else" (p. 4).

To help offset these anticipated difficulties, Ann involved the students in selecting the books they were to read, provided students with a unit calendar, and planned at least two distinctly different activities each day. During a typical class period, students spent the first 10 minutes writing in their Dialogue Journals, the next 20 minutes meeting with their book clubs, and the final 20 minutes working on a create-a-character project (see page 27).

As she debated about whether to teach a unit focusing on multicultural literature, Ann often called me at night to discuss articles related to multicultural literature and its teaching. Twice she attempted to contact her school district's diversity coordinator but was unable to get specific assistance or feedback. After much consideration and soul searching, Ann decided to move ahead. She spent three weeks designing and preparing to teach the unit. Because of her teaching load, this preparation was done while she was teaching other units. Still, she carefully designed assignments to achieve her goals, and she prepared to involve her students in deciding which novels to read.

Selecting and Obtaining the Literature

Because Ann knew that students react more positively to texts they have had a part in choosing, she involved them in the selection process. First, students helped select six novels and then chose one of the six novels to read. Students who read the same novels worked together in groups, or book clubs, to prepare presentations through which they shared what they had read with the class. In describing how novels for the unit were selected, Ann said,

> I considered the following carefully: appeal/interest level (including gender of the protagonist), ability level (high/middle/low), variety in cultures, and authenticity of the author. Unfortunately, another factor I had to consider was cost, so I had to have books available in paperback, which eliminated a few excellent choices. I looked at lists of recommended multicultural novels recommended for this age level, spoke to Dr. Dressel, and read 10 books and parts of another 5.

Ann selected 10 potential titles:

1. *Waiting for the Rain: A Novel of South Africa* by Sheila Gordon (1987)

2. *Finding My Voice* by Marie G. Lee (1992)

3. *Shabanu: Daughter of the Wind* by Suzanne Fisher Staples (1989)

4. *Journey of the Sparrows* by Fran Leeper Buss with Daisy Cubias (1991)

5. *Scorpions* by Walter Dean Myers (1988)

6. *Shadow of the Dragon* by Sherry Garland (1993)

7. *Letters of a Slave Girl* by Mary Lyons (1992)

8. *To Spoil the Sun* by Joyce Rockwood (1976)

9. *Annie John* by Jamaica Kincaid (1985)

10. *Year of Impossible Goodbyes* by Sook Nyul Choi (1991)

Ann had not been able to obtain a firm commitment from the school principal to pay for the books. So, she drafted a letter to the parents of her students, sharing her goals for the unit, explaining that students would need to write in the books, and asking parents to help underwrite the cost. But she never had to send the letter. In order to keep the school administration informed about her classroom activities and to ensure the support of the school district for the multicultural unit, Ann met with her principal to request permission to send the letter. The principal, confronted with the letter, committed to purchasing the books but cautioned Ann to keep the cost under $500.

For the final selection process, Ann devised a ballot for students to use to vote on the books, and she included a two-line description of each book on the ballot. She noted in her journal, "I deliberately did not put the titles of the novels on the survey because I wanted the students to choose based on the reality as opposed to their misinterpretation of the title." Using the following ballot, students in all four classes voted on the books they wanted to include in the unit:

Ballot to Determine Novels Read During Unit

Our next unit is a book club unit in which you will be asked to select and read a book in a group of up to five students. To help determine the list of six to seven books from which you will choose, please read the following short summaries of books. Based on that information, please label the list 1 through 10, with 1 being the one you're most interested in reading and 10 being the one you're least interested in reading. Use each number only once. Thank you for your input.

- __ Story about three kids from El Salvador who come to Chicago illegally, in a crate, to try to make a better life for themselves and their family.

- __ True story about a black slave who plans to escape to the North during the period before the Civil War. Describes what slavery was really like.

- __ Story about a black guy who lives on the streets in New York City and his struggles with family problems, poverty, gangs, and violence.

- __ Story about a teen who grows up in a nomadic family in Pakistan. She faces family problems and deals with an arranged marriage that she doesn't want.

- __ Story about two Vietnamese teens, one who struggles to fit into midwestern America after living in refugee camps, and one who struggles to balance his double identity as Vietnamese and American.

_‡_ Story about a Cherokee Indian of southern Florida, showing her world and how the coming of the Europeans destroyed her tribe by bringing smallpox.

_·_ Story of two guys (one black and one white) who grew up together in South Africa. It tells the story of apartheid and their friendship.

___ Story of a black girl growing up in Antigua (British West Indies) and her issues with herself and her parents as she prepares to be on her own.

___ Story of a Korean family and their struggle during the communist occupation of Korea, their fight to protect women from sexual abuse, and their search for freedom and peace for their family.

_·_ Story about a Chinese American* girl living in Hibbing, Minnesota, and her struggles with school, teachers, peers, boyfriends, and parents during her senior year of high school.

*Note: This story is about Korean Americans, not Chinese Americans. The teacher caught this mistake later, and the implications are discussed in chapter 4.

The students in each class ranked the books from 1 to 10. Ann originally planned to use the seven books that garnered the most points. When ordering the books, however, she was unable to obtain a paperback edition of one title, so she ended up with six books. But, shortly after ordering the books, *Morning Girl* (Dorris,1992) was recommended to her by the head of the special education department who felt the book would be appropriate for Ann's mainstreamed special education students. Thus, *Morning Girl* became the seventh book in the following final selection:

- *Waiting for the Rain: A Novel of South Africa*
- *Finding My Voice*
- *Shabanu: Daughter of the Wind*
- *Journey of the Sparrows*
- *Scorpions*
- *Shadow of the Dragon*
- *Morning Girl*

When the novels arrived, Ann again involved the students in the selection process. She passed the novels around to the students as they sat in a circle on the floor so they could get an idea of the contents. After looking through the books, each student listed his or her top three choices on the ballot. Ann promised the students that they would get to read one of their top three choices, and, except for the special education students in the class who all read *Morning Girl*, she kept her promise to all the students. When it was time for students to evaluate the unit, their comments indicated that they valued their participation in the selection of the novels for a variety of reasons. For example, when asked from which assignment they felt they learned the most, Perry and Dee responded that they learned the most from being able to choose the books they read. Perry said he felt that way "because you could choose which book you had the most interest in." Dee said "choosing the book" was most important "because I learned about something I didn't know much about."

The Assignments

During the actual unit, students completed various assignments. The Pre-Unit Survey (see Appendix C) was completed by students before the unit began. On the survey, Ann asked how students felt about reading new novels and novels with characters who had different backgrounds and histories from their own. She asked the students to identify the positive and negative things they knew about different groups of people. She asked them where they had learned these things and how they knew the information was accurate. The Post-Unit Survey (see Appendix D), the same survey except with two changes, was repeated at the end of the unit. First, students were asked how they felt about reading their specific novels rather than new novels in general. Second, they were asked whether they would choose to read another novel with characters who had backgrounds and histories different from their own. Ann did not grade the surveys, but students received points toward their unit grade if the surveys were completed.

In each class, students reading the same novel met together in book clubs. In the book clubs, students worked together on the Book Club Organizer and an oral group project that grew out of the work they did on their organizers. Although Ann tried to create groups that were gender balanced and heterogeneous, a few were all male or all female because of the students' book selections.

According to Ann, the Book Club Organizer (see Figure 1 and Appendix A) was designed

> to give students a place to keep track of their novel and to give some shape to their club's discussion time. It was also a way to have the students gain more practice and expertise with literary elements: setting and point of view, plot line, character list, conflict, culture and stereotypes, symbols, and theme.

Responses were graded for completeness, accuracy, and insight.

Figure 1. Book Club Organizer

Directions: This packet is designed to help your Book Club keep track of its novel by providing a place for you to jot down different information about the novel.

Name of the novel: *Finding my Voice.*
Author of the novel: *Marie G. Lee*
Book Club Members:

Setting: Describe the setting(s) of the novel, including cultural specifics

Arkin, a small town in Minnesota. Mostly Scandanavian community, not many orientals. Takes place mostly at Arkin High School & the main characters home.

Point of View: Tell what point of view the author has chosen, define that point of view, and give several reasons why the author might have chosen that narrator.

She chose first person, which means that she writes as if she was the main character. It tells you more about Ellen's thoughts & feelings than any other would have told. In other words, if she had chosen 2nd or 3rd person

By its very nature, the organizer encouraged students to operate out of an efferent stance to the literature. Comments from students' evaluations of the unit indicate that they understood the purpose of the organizer and recognized that it helped them recall and organize information:

Steve: [It's] easier to remember if [it's] on a peice of paper.

Ralph: It helps to organize certain notes.

Jason: I wrote down a lot of info.

Megan: [It] made you find out details.

Lisa:	Because you could put all the information about what was going on.
Ken:	[Because] I had to remember carefully everything that happened.
Bill:	It was there if I forgot something that was important.
Alan:	Because we were writing down what we learned.
Sheila:	Because as I wrote things down, I had a chance to absorb and understand more clearly.
Eric:	[Because] you had to really think about what you read.
Amanda:	[The] Book Club Organizer made me think about things I don't normally think about when I read a book.

For the Dialogue Journal assignment (see Appendix B), students worked with partners. Partners read different books so that they would learn about two cultures different from their own. In her journal, Ann noted that in addition to learning about the characteristics of different cultures, a second purpose of the Dialogue Journal was to help students understand what it meant to live as a member of a particular culture. She explained that she wanted students to take the point of view of one of the characters in their novels, to try to see the world from a different cultural perspective.

The journal entries took the form of letters (see Figure 2), and journals were evaluated holistically, based on completeness and thoughtfulness; both the journaler and the responder received points. Most of the students who identified this assignment as the one from which they learned the most said it was because of the opportunity to learn about two books, two lifestyles, two viewpoints, or two characters. Three students, though, actually commented on the interactive process of teaching and learning involved in the dialoguing. Pete explained, "I was teaching what I knew and was geting taught what [Donald] knew," while Taffy said that the Dialogue Journal "helped sort things through with someone else." Only one student, Paula, made any direct comment about the cultural component of the learning. She found "writing in the Dialogue Journal [most helpful because] I learned about other cultures and conflicts of others."

The book club projects were designed to enable members of each book club to communicate to their classmates what they learned from reading their books. Students were not to retell the story but were to focus on conflicts, culture, characters, symbols, or themes. There was a variety of presentation

Figure 2. Dialogue Journal

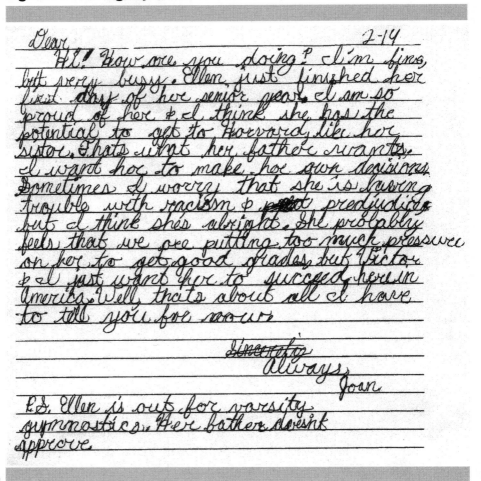

formats from which to choose: newspaper, children's book, poetry book, comic strip, television talk show, news broadcast, press conference, museum exhibit, or puppet show. Each group member received the same grade; content was worth 60% and creativity 40%. At the end of the project, group members individually evaluated one another's group skills, and based on those evaluations Ann awarded up to 25 additional points. After each group's presentation, other class members identified three things they learned from the presentation. Ideally, the presentations were to function as a way for students to learn something about all the cultures represented in the novels. However, of all the assignments, this one was the most disappointing to Ann. She didn't feel the students "learned anything by watching the presentations." She wrote,

> The most glaring evidence of students' inability to deal with cultural differences effectively was found in their book club projects, which lacked insight and depth…. Because they were unable to go beyond the factual events of the novel[s] to think about what their significance might be, they were unable to communicate adequately about the different cultural groups; for example, *Shabanu* was only about arranged Pakistani marriages, and *Scorpions* was only about guns and blacks in the city.

Although Ann felt as though she had failed her students, her students didn't agree. In their evaluations of the unit, the students' opinions stood in stark contrast to Ann's evaluation. Out of the nine activities Ann listed, 44 students—40%—felt they had learned the most from the book club project. Only the Book Club Organizer came close, with 21 students—less than 20%. Although only 2 students said specifically that they liked the project because it was fun, many of the students implied they had enjoyed it. Tom was quite articulate in his response. In describing the value of the book club project, he said, "doing book club project…was fun and you learn more when you enjoy what you are doing." Many students explained that part of the enjoyment they felt came from working together. They also felt that hearing from others was valuable. They wrote that working together made them think and helped them to learn, both individually and from others. For example, Sissy explained that "during the final project I had to put together a 'summary' of the whole unit and share it with the class. It made me think of what I learned." Julie, too, testified that "you had to think more." Chuck said that the most learning occurred in the book club project "because it tested all we knew about the book." And Marina expressed the same idea when she said, "We really got to the point of the story [when we did the project]." The need to integrate ideas in order to present them to others was important to many students. For example, Ellen found the book club project valuable "because you put it together yourself after reading in other words, you put together what you learned." Katie echoed this when she shared that when "doing the project everything that we learned from the book had to be put into one big thing."

Although many students mentioned critical thinking and the integration of ideas, even more of them commented on the value of the close interaction of peers, both in working together and in sharing ideas. Tasha and Toby found value in the interactive aspects of completing the organizer. Tasha said, "The project gave me a good chance to comunicate what I had learned," and Toby felt that he "learned other perspectives of what the group saw in the book." The reasons they gave for finding the book club project valuable reflected the value they found in cooperative learning:

Jody: [Our] group put all our ideas together so you learned more.

Alicia: [We] used team work and understood everyones ideas and sugestions about the book.

Paul: You put all your ideas together.

Nathan: It put a lot of things together and also allowed us to share ideas.

Rebecca: I got things other people saw in the book.

Charles: Our group worked good and they taught me a lot. I learned more in this because it's easier in a group.

Howie: We all got to share what we learned.

Joey: We all cooperated and had a good time.

Jill: We had to be creative, listen, and think.

Many students found the book club project valuable because it extended their learning about cultures. Rather than only learning about the cultures reflected in the one book they read, many students indicated the value they found in learning about additional cultures from their peers. The following comments were common:

Brett: It taught me a lot about other people.

Chrys: I learn more on how they live from talking to group members.

Matt: I learned about many books.

Donny: [It] gives an in-depth view of other cultures.

Karen: We did a lot dealing with cultures.

Terry: I learned about there books.

Ginny: I learned about a book I never read.

Pam: I learned thing about different cultures.

During the reading of the novels, students completed two other long-term assignments that were tangentially related to the unit: the thinkbook and the create-a-character project. I did not have access to either. Ann described the thinkbooks as "personal teacher/student dialogue journals."

Throughout the year, students wrote in their thinkbooks for the first 10 minutes of class, and Ann responded in writing once a week. As the researcher, I thought this written assignment was more likely to contain information important to the study. However, because I found that students often shared similar, if not identical, responses in the other writing I examined, I found that not having access to the thinkbooks may not have been as problematic as I first thought. For example, Ann wrote in her journal,

> I enjoyed reading the thinkbooks last week. There was a question about what they have learned from their book and if they like it, and some kids really seem to have been positively affected. Eric—perhaps my brightest student—said his book has made him see the complexities of immigration issues. He said he didn't have a solution, but that these people need help and also shouldn't be illegal. I thought it was very positive for him to be thinking about these things.

Eric shared similar responses in his Book Club Organizer and Dialogue Journal when he said,

> illegal aliens have worse lives than we think and that they do deserve a chance in America. They have many risks coming here but are brave enough to come anyway.

And, when he assumed the identity of Maria (*Journey of the Sparrows*), he reflected,

> I sometimes contemplate my future. I think that my life won't get any better from now on but instead stay the same maybe even get worse...I fear we will be caught.... The hardships [portrayed in the book] are really the truth...it shows how we have to work harder than most.

The create-a-character project was another lengthy assignment. Students were to create a human character with a complete history. Because they were to create an entire life for the character, Ann suggested that it would be more interesting if the character were an adult. From a list of possible activities, students had to select and create 20 items relating to their character's life (e.g., a birth certificate, a family tree, a comparison of themselves to the character, or a letter from the character to his or her mother). Although the assignment was tedious and time-consuming to evaluate, Ann knew students in previous classes had enjoyed it and felt that it fit especially well with the multicultural unit because students would be exposed to new possibilities and a variety of lifestyles in their reading. She hoped that students would incorporate some of what they learned from their novels into decisions they made and the stories they created about their characters. Although Ann encouraged students to apply what they learned in their novels about character development to the development of their own characters, she did not require it. She felt there was disappointingly little carry-over in students' learning from the multicultural novels to the create-a-character project.

The Research

As researcher, my role was to examine students' written work and to determine if they had achieved the objectives Ann had established for the multicultural unit. Because this was not an experimental study, students were not randomly selected nor was there any attempt to implement any procedures or methods other than those Ann chose to use: As during the rest of the year, students remained in their normal classes, and Ann designed and taught the unit. Of 123 students, the written work of 32 students in one class was used to create an evaluation instrument (see Appendix E), and the written work of the remaining 91 students was evaluated using that instrument.

As I examined the Pre- and Post-Unit Surveys on attitudes and knowledge, the Book Club Organizer, and the Dialogue Journal, I used the following questions to assess whether students had met Ann's objectives:

- Did they enjoy reading and understanding their multicultural novels?
- Did they learn about the norms and values of a culture different from their own, and if so, what did they learn?
- Did they come to understand themselves, their cultural values, and their cultural norms more clearly?

The Pre- and Post-Unit Surveys were similar, the Post-Unit Survey being a modified version of the Pre-Unit Survey. Both surveys asked students to identify, before and after reading, the positive and negative things they knew or believed about the people—South African, Pakistani, Chinese American, African American, Latino American, Vietnamese American, and Korean American—reflected in the novels read during the unit. After identifying the positives and negatives for each group, students were asked, "Where did you learn that?" and "How do you know all this information is accurate?" At the end of both surveys, Ann asked the students to define the word *culture* and to "name as many unique characteristics of your culture as you can." Because readers answered these questions before and after participating in the unit and the assignments, I was able to compare their answers and determine whether their answers had changed.

As previously noted, the Book Club Organizer encouraged readers to assume an efferent stance to their reading. It was designed to focus students' attention on the text. An important aspect of this assignment was that students worked in groups. They contracted with their group about reading due dates at which times they discussed the story. Following the discussion, they completed a fairly traditional assignment sheet that asked about the literary elements. In addition to these traditional literary components, students also were asked about the culture portrayed in the book. They were asked what they learned about the worlds the characters lived in, what was valued in those worlds, what the characters believed in, and how that compared or contrasted with their own worlds. Ann also asked students to identify stereotypes that were "promoted" and "destroyed" in the novel. Finally, they were asked to explain why they felt the novel was, or was not, an authentic representation of the particular culture.

For the Dialogue Journal assignment, readers were paired with a partner who read a different book and each partner created a journal. Journalers assumed the identity of a character in their books and carried on written conversations with their partners. Partners responded as themselves. This assignment encouraged an aesthetic stance to literature. It asked readers to participate in virtual experiences, which were guided by the text but created by individual readers in light of their own cognitive and affective responses to their reading. From the Dialogue Journals, I was able to determine what happened when dominant-culture readers "became" characters from nondominant cultures.

Finally, I looked for evidence in all assignments that would indicate whether the students exhibited any problem behaviors Ann anticipated:

- Did they create generalizations about all members of a cultural group based on the cultural group in their novel?

- Did they accept the presentation of the cultural group without questioning the novel or the author?

- Did they judge characters from a nondominant group using dominant (western-European American) cultural standards?

- Did they ignore or not recognize the impact that being a member of a nondominant culture had on the lives of the characters?

- Did they see characters from nondominant cultures as "victims" rather than as people with a whole range of human experience?
- Did they need more teacher guidance and assistance than Ann was able to provide in the book club unit?

I expected that the degree to which the students participated in these behaviors would help shed light on how they perceived people different from themselves.

Creating the Evaluation Instrument

To develop the questions for the Evaluation Instrument, I used the assignments completed by Ann's third-period class. As I read and reread the papers, I began to notice patterns and particulars that appeared over and over. For example, I began to notice that students seemed to think that Korean nationals and Korean Americans were the same. Because this was clearly the kind of information that would help me to determine whether readers had or had not met Ann's goals, I designed a question to determine whether readers had made this assumption: Does the reader appear to recognize that Korean American and Korean are different, that African American and African are different, etc.?

When the question was asked of the rest of the third-period papers and I found that I could answer it, the question was included in the final questionnaire. Although this is an interesting example, the development and testing of the questions was quite difficult. It took nearly three months before I was confident that the questions would actually provide valid information. For the final instrument, I settled on 29 different questions. However, 15 questions would have to be answered about multiple assignments, making 44 total questions that scorers would have to answer about each student's set of assignments (see Appendix E).

During the process of refining the questions, I also developed a detailed Rubric for Training Raters (see Appendix F). The rubric contained an explanation of each question and a description of its intent. When the Evaluation Instrument was completed, I used the rubric to train a second independent rater. Because the nature of the decisions demanded by the questions required intense concentration, this rubric became an invaluable reference as student papers were examined. First, using the rubric as a guide, we scored student papers independently and then compared our results. The process was continued until we were confident that the questions were being interpreted in the same way. The papers from students in Ann's third-period class were used as practice papers, and because they were used to develop the instrument and standard-ize scoring, they could not be included in the actual evaluation. This left 91 sets of papers: 27 from period four, 31 from period five, and 33 from period six. Each set of student papers contained 20 to 25 pages of handwritten material and took approximately one hour per set to evaluate. Independently of each other, both raters scored all papers. It took approximately four months for each rater to complete the scoring.

When the scoring was completed, I noticed some unusual discrepancies. For example, Jill was labeled *female* by one evaluator and *male* by the other; on another paper, the book read was misidentified by one evaluator but not by the other. It quickly became obvious that such discrepancies were caused by the amount of material and the intensity involved in analyzing it. To remedy this, each rater reread all items on which there was disagreement to decide if the original decision was indeed the one we wanted. Even if we had wanted to do so, we could not have obtained agreement just by changing our answers, because some items had four, five, or six options from which to choose. Even on items where the answers were yes or no, one scorer had no way of knowing whether the other scorer's response would stay the same. I consulted two statisticians who agreed that the reliability of the scoring was not compromised. Because the only option was to make an independent decision, the integrity of inde-pendent scoring was maintained.

The relationship between scores of independent raters is called reliability. When raters read papers separately and their scores agree, we say the reliabili-ty is high. As raters, we had worked together until the reliability between our scores, when we scored the practice papers independently, was very high. However, the only thing that mattered in the long run was the scoring of the re-maining papers. For this scoring, we couldn't talk to one another or compare our thinking or our answers. This part of the scoring had to be totally inde-pendent or no one would trust the findings. The findings would be reliable only if both of us found the same thing independently of each other. So, once the scoring was complete, I had to compute the interrater reliability for the pa-pers of students in the three remaining classes. We did agree. The interrater reliability for all items was statistically significant and ranged from .7 to 1.0, with the exception of items number 17 and number 26 on the Evaluation Instrument. The interrater reliabilities for these were .53 and .63, respectively. A high interrater reliability means that, separately, both raters had made the same decision about a large number of questions.

Because actual student work was used to develop the questions used to analyze student papers, it is likely that the evaluation instrument actually measures what it is supposed to measure. If so, that means that what researchers call the validity of the scoring instrument is high. When the reliability is high and the validity is high, the results can be considered accurate.

It is again important to note that I analyzed only written assignments in this study. Had I explored students' oral responses, it is possible that the results might have been different. Perhaps they would not have been, though. Peggy Rice (1999) found similar results when she analyzed the oral responses of eight white, "mid-to-high middle-class"(p. 2) sixth graders who were capable readers and who had experience discussing literature in peer discussion groups: Students' cultural affiliations provided the base for their interpretations of words, meanings, and ideas.

In this study, as in Rice's, students' cultural affiliations influenced their responses to and understanding of literature. Although parents and students in this middle SES community acknowledged Ann as an outstanding teacher, although Ann recognized that it was important for students to respond personally to literature and to think critically about culture as it is reflected in literature, and although she was conscientious in planning the unit—even involving students in selecting the literature—other influences were also present. In addition to Ann's teaching, the students' writing clearly reflected the influence of previous years of schooling and the media as well as the culture of the local and ethnic community to which they belonged. In the next chapters, I'll look at these influences and how they interacted.

CHAPTER 2

Responding to Literature

> *Two kids came up to me this morning and said their books were the best books they've ever read! Undoubtedly, the most positive part of this unit was the enjoyment the students derived from the novels. (Ann)*

Rosenblatt (1938/1976) argues that the kind of response Ann saw in her students—their spontaneous response to literature—is absolutely essential and that it is the first step in any reading of literature. Having this kind of response was Ann's first and primary goal for her students, but she hadn't expected her students to respond as positively as they did. In the journal she kept while teaching the unit, Ann reflected,

> I had been led to believe by some colleagues that students generally do not like multicultural fiction, [but] I did not find that to be the case at all. Several students asked me personally for recommendations of other books "like this one" and, according to the surveys, the large majority enjoyed the book they read or at least liked it as well as other books they have read.

Participating in an aesthetic transaction with literature was an important component and a main objective of Ann's unit. Carole Cox and Joyce Many (1992) explain that "what's important in a literature-based approach is to acknowledge and celebrate each reader's responses...[to] take experiences with literature beyond choosing to create individual versions of reality...[and] centering the literature teaching experience in the literary responses of readers" (pp. 122–124). In research they conducted with fourth through eighth graders, Cox and Many found that students who become personally involved in a story obtained higher levels of understanding than students who responded efferently. When examining the effects of teaching on response to literature, Joyce Many and Donna Wiseman (1992) found that the teacher's approach to teaching literature affected the responses of both elementary children and preservice teachers. When the teachers encouraged students to focus on personal associations and feelings evoked by literature, on empathizing with story characters, and on relating powerful images evoked, they found that students responded with what Purves called *personal significance*—personal reactions unique to the individual reader. Efferent approaches in which the teachers encouraged the students to focus on literary elements of the stories such as character, plot, and theme development were more likely to result in students focusing on understandings of the works created by communities of readers—what Purves called *shared* or *cultural significance*. Individual readers tended to hold back their own opinions, responding in a more formal way and referring less to their own personal responses.

Rogers (1991), too, found strong evidence that students' preferences for ways of interpreting literature were affected by the way teachers taught. After students had participated in sessions in which they were expected to assume a larger role in interpreting the literature and expected to incorporate references to multiple "texts," including comparisons to characters in other texts and to personal responses, students tended to prefer this style of interpretation over interpretation that focused on textual elements of a story during which the teacher possessed the social and interpretive authority.

Responses of Readers

When I analyzed the written responses of the students, I discovered that Ann's feeling about her students enjoying their books was accurate. In fact, if the responses of Ann's students are typical of the responses of white readers, teachers shouldn't pay attention to people who say that children don't like multicultural literature. We have known for a long time that readers like well-written and interesting literature. The writing of Ann's students indicates that their responses to well-written, interesting multicultural literature are no different. These findings aren't unique, though. Ostrowski (1997) discovered that when teachers used multicultural literature, they found that their students responded to cultural literature just as they did to other literature. They often were more interested in whether they could relate to it than they were in the cultural issues. Even though Ann's students were asked to do a significant amount of work during the unit, she received few complaints about it. Normally, students would have complained that the work was too hard, there was too much of it, or that it was no fun. She wrote, "Even the Book Club Organizer, the type of thing they generally dislike, seemed to be regarded as a necessary evil and, therefore, tolerable." The assignments the students completed provide concrete evidence that they did, indeed, like their books. Because students were never specifically asked if they liked their books, it wasn't possible to answer the question directly. But it was possible to look for evidence that would indicate that they didn't like their books. Neither of the two independent evaluators found any. In the 69 Book Club Organizers turned in, there was no evidence to indicate that a student did not enjoy reading the book. Of 75 Dialogue Journals, 73 (97.3%) contained no evidence of dislike, and of 68 Post-Unit Surveys, 64 (94.1%) contained no such evidence.

Before beginning the unit, Ann asked students, "How do you usually feel about reading a new novel?" Of the 91 students, 83 responded (8 did not complete the assignment). Of these, 40% indicated that they generally looked forward to reading new novels; 10% had negative feelings about having to read a new novel; 20% didn't care one way or the other; and 25% indicated that either they didn't like to read, had trouble reading, or didn't like to read school-assigned material. After the unit, Ann asked students a similar question but this time inquired about the specific novels they read: "How did you feel about reading this novel?" After students read multicultural novels, 83% of the 69 papers turned in reflected their positive feelings. In statistical terms, this change was highly significant ($p < .0001$). Only 4% of students responded negatively, while 15.7% were neutral. Astonishingly enough, none mentioned they didn't like to read, had trouble reading, or didn't like to read school-assigned material. It's clear from these numbers that the students liked reading their multicultural books, and when I looked more closely at the results, I discovered additional information.

Readers Who Like to Read New Novels

In the Pre-Unit Surveys, 34 students responded positively when asked how they felt about reading a new novel. Of those 34, 29 students turned in Post-Unit Surveys, and 27 of the 29 expressed the same or greater enthusiasm after reading their multicultural novels. For example, Kathy was a student who liked to read. Before the unit, when asked how she felt about reading a new novel, she replied, "I am usually curious about a new novel. I'm not very picky when it comes to what kind of novel. My curiosity get's the better of me and I get interested. Sometimes I find that a book may have a boring title, but is[n't] really." After reading *Shadow of the Dragon*, she enthusiastically shared, "I felt good about myself when I read this novel. I learned new things about a different culture and it was a very good book, too."

Before the unit, another student, Eric, said he felt "excited, because I like to read and learn new things." After reading his multicultural novel, he exclaimed, "I felt great because it told me about the problems of others." Ted looked forward to reading novels, too. He explained, "I feel good because I don't read a lot and it makes me read more and [if] I have to do it for class I will do it." After reading his multicultural novel, Ted answered, "I felt good about this novel because I learned lots of new thing that I didn't before."

The remaining two readers who reported on their Pre-Unit Surveys that they felt positively about reading new novels weren't necessarily enthusiastic, but even these two didn't have bad experiences. Before reading, Tim noted, "I enjoy reading so I don't really care, just as long as its remotely interesting," but he added, "I don't like reading about other background because I don't easily understand everything, like I do with our background." Robert shared, "I think it's fun, but sometimes hard because you don't remember everything," and he added, "I like reading novels like that because I learn about their cultures and it usualy makes the novel interesting." Tim and Robert were in different classes, but both read *Shadow of the Dragon*. After finishing the book, both boys explained their responses in terms of what they learned, but with very different results. Tim replied, "I didn't really learn anything from this because I was already aware that this happens a lot." He said that "[in the future, I wouldn't choose to read another novel whose characters have a different background and history from mine] because I like to read things I can identify with (e.g., Baseball books, etc.)." Robert said, "I felt OK. I didn't know some things I know now." But, unlike Tim, Robert said, "Yes, [in the future, I would choose to read another novel whose characters have a different background and history from mine because] I like reading about other cultures."

Readers Who Do Not Like to Read New Novels

It was not only Ann's enthusiastic readers who enjoyed the multicultural novels but also her less enthusiastic readers. These readers didn't specifically object to reading per se, but they certainly didn't look forward to reading a new novel. Ostrowski (1997) notes that sometimes students read merely because they want to pass a test: "Simply getting students to read anything, according to several of the teachers in our study, is one of the greatest challenges they face" (p. 63). Students in Ann's classes were no different. When previewing their books to decide which one they most wanted to read, some students were quite blunt about wanting the shortest book, and some even resorted to counting pages.

There were seven readers who simply did not like reading new novels. Three did not turn in a Post-Unit Survey, so we don't know how they felt about reading their novel, but because of other work they turned in, we do know that at least two did read their books. Of four students who did turn in the survey, none were negative about the experience of reading their multicultural novels. In fact, two students, Steve and John, had changed their minds completely. Before the unit, Steve said, "I don't like to read them, most of them get boring," but he changed his mind after reading *Journey of the Sparrows*. He candidly explained, "Well, at first I wasn't sure [how I felt]. But now I read I'm glad I did." John doesn't mention being bored but reflected thoughtfully, "I usually feel discourged because I don't think that I can read that much, and I don't think that I would like it. I don't know, I guess I don't give books a chance." However, after giving *Finding My Voice* a chance, Steve was emphatic: "It is a good novel and I was compelled to read it. I loved it and finished it in two days."

The two remaining responses were somewhat different. At the beginning, Greg felt that reading novels was a burden. He described it this way: "I feel like there is a ton on my back way behind and when I have to read more there is 21½ more tons." After reading *Morning Girl*, his response was not positive, but his description of content was less negative than his earlier objection: "I felt the author was telling the readers about how it was on an island and what to exspect on an island in 1675 or something." Ronnie, the last reader who was negative about reading novels, didn't object to reading itself but said, "I usually don't like reading new novels because half of the books I read are stupid. But if people tell me its really good, I'll try it." He was still negative after reading his novel but for a very different reason. He made no reference to *Scorpions* being stupid, but he objected to the image of blacks that he felt emerged from the book. He said, "I really don't know how I feel. I guess I didn't really like how they made Blacks look." Although Ronnie said he would not choose to read another multicultural novel, his response is actually a hopeful sign in relation to Ann's goals, because, rather than objecting to reading, he is now questioning the portrayal of the cultural group reflected in the novel.

Eighteen readers did not have strong feelings either way about reading novels at the beginning of the unit. Of these readers, 16 turned in Post-Unit Surveys: 80% were no longer lukewarm; in fact, they definitely liked their multicultural novels. These readers were thoughtful in explaining their reasons. For example, before the unit, Noah said, "I am usually a little aprehensive [about reading a new novel] because I am worried about the subject matter," but his relief is almost palpable when he decided, after finishing *Journey of the Sparrows*, "I thought it was a very good book. I would not complain about reading it [on] my own." Bill made a special effort to explain that his response changed a number of times while he was reading: "At first, before I started reading it, I thought it would be neat to read about someone traveling in a crate but then I hated the book until about 1/4 of the way through then I started liking it." T.J., a member of a nondominant culture, wrote about *Finding My Voice*: "It was very sad because it is true that people don't like you because you look different." Amy admitted about *Scorpions* that she was "skeptial at first but when I started reading it a lot, I liked it a lot. I think you just have to get involved with it somehow." And *Shabanu* "was fun [and] interesting" for Taffy because she "learned something new from it." Four students, two of whom read *Waiting for the Rain*, were still indifferent after the unit. Sue replied that she "felt normal. It wasn't the best book I ever read, but it was pretty good. It could have more details." Megan felt that "it got more interesting towards the end. It could have been more interesting but I guess it was okay." The other two students both read *Journey of the Sparrows*. One said, "It was just another book about immigrants coming to the U.S.," and one commented very honestly, "I didn't really have a feeling about reading this book. It was an assignment so I did it."

Students Who Simply Do Not Like to Read

An especially interesting finding had to do with a select group of students who made it clear on their Pre-Unit Surveys that they didn't like to read at all, that they had trouble reading, or that they simply didn't like to read teacher-assigned material or to do the assignments afterward. One quarter of all the students who turned in their initial surveys fell into this group. Of these students, 80% turned in their Post-Unit Surveys and, amazingly, after reading their multicultural novels, more than 75% liked reading their novels. There were no comments about not liking reading, about having difficulty reading, or about objecting to assigned books or to the assignments related to the unit. It was obvious that these students, too, liked reading the multicultural literature. Roger, a mainstreamed special education student, said, about reading a new novel, that he felt "sad because I don't read fast and can never keep up with the other class." After reading *Morning Girl*, not only did he feel better, but he also evaluated the novel, saying he felt "alright, it was a good book but [there wasn't] much to it," and indicating that he would choose to read another one like it. Liz, also a special education student who read *Morning Girl*, said she felt "stupid" about reading a new novel, "because I don't like the books. I would rather pice [pick] my own book out." After finishing the novel, she felt "OK because I liked when she collect shells because I love collect shells," and Liz, too, would choose to read another multicultural novel.

It was not only the special education students who disliked reading novels at the beginning of the unit. Bob, a student who did not like to read, explained, "I don't want to [read new novels]. I don't like reading." After reading *Waiting for the Rain*, he still said, "I do not like to read," but, he continued, "this was a good book with good subject matter." Katie revealed, "I think reading a new novel is kind of different and boring. The reason why is because I really don't like to read that much but I will." By the time she finished reading *Scorpions*, she was able to say, "I liked reading this novel because it gave me a little bit more knowledge about Black people." Sandra, a particularly articulate student, said she often felt "disappointed" about reading a new novel because "I have just finished a really good book and I don't know about the book and how good it is. For school, it really isn't fun because if you don't like the book, you can't pick a new one." However, after reading *Shabanu*, Sandra acknowledged, "I liked this novel a lot because it was very exciting and the characters sounded real. They had thier own thoughts and she made them exciting. It had a lot of action and it also didn't get very boring." Maureen was one of the students who didn't like to read teacher-assigned material. She insisted, "I like reading on my own time with my own book better than a novel in class. It's more fun, because it's the type of book I like and I don't have to worry about remembering every last detail." However, similar to Sandra, she enjoyed *Shabanu*, too, because "it was interesting and I enjoyed the story."

Chuck, who liked the action in *Shadow of the Dragon*, said, "I don't like novels because you're reading about the same topic/subject for a long time. Also if I have to read a novel I want to have heard about it before." After reading his book, though, he felt as Sandra did about *Shabanu*: "It was interesting, lots of action scenerios." Gil, a second-generation Asian American, simply noted, "Honestly I don't realy like to read. Once in a while I get a book that is realy interasting but I only see a couple of those," but after reading *Shadow of the Dragon*, he said, "I liked the novel because I could relate to it." Finally, Dan, who didn't want to read new novels because he didn't like to read very much, summed it all up in a few words: "I feel like reading this novel was fun."

The issue of simply getting students to read anything was an important one for Ann. Of the 16 students who didn't turn in their Dialogue Journals, at least 10 were very poor readers. In *You Gotta BE the Book*, Wilhelm (1997) writes about the differences between what expert readers and poor readers do and do not do when they read and about what teachers can do to help. Wilhelm describes how he scrapped the idea of teaching literature as content and, instead, after reading a text together as a class, he involved his students in teaching one another how to read the literature. The literature became the vehicle through which readers learned about one another's strategies and, in sharing strategies, learned about the literature. Although Wilhelm's ultimate goal was to help readers reach what Rosenblatt (1978) calls a "valid" (p. 115) reading—one that accounts for as many of the elements in the text as possible and, at the same time, doesn't imply things which aren't in the text—his primary function with poorer readers was to help them recognize their need to be active in creating meaning. With expert readers, he found "multicultural literature, in particular, help[ed] students to enter other perspectives" (Wilhelm, 1997, p. 35). But entering another's perspective is a richer way of reading to which many poorer readers don't have access because it "depends upon first having built a story world that depends in large part on associating real-life experiences with textual clues" (p. 48).

Although many educators acknowledge that an aesthetic response is a necessary prerequisite to interpreting and reflecting on the world of the story, Wilhelm's thrust is that poorer readers have never been taught "how to evoke and enter a secondary world" (p. 99). Instead, his students understood reading to be the decoding of words and expected the text to give them the answers. When it did not, it reinforced students' reluctance to read, their negative attitudes toward reading, and their perceptions of themselves as poor readers. He states, "I think it was an important finding that none of the less engaged readers ever responded on the connective or reflective response dimensions unless they had first fully evoked and experienced the world of the story" (p. 144). One technique he found helpful in this regard was story drama, which requires readers to respond to a situation or conflict from a character's viewpoint. This appeared to assist poorer readers in re-creating a secondary world and resulted in them "enjoy[ing] the experience of literature" (p. 112). In advocating artistic-response activities, Wilhelm (1997) quotes Elliot Eisner (1992), "We cannot know through language what we cannot imagine. The image—visual, tactile, auditory—plays a crucial role in the construction of meaning through text. Those who cannot imagine cannot read (p. 125)," and,

Wilhelm adds, "according to my classroom experience, don't want to" (p. 120). In this vein, it is not surprising that none of the reluctant readers in Wilhelm's study remembered being read to much, and none of them had "any memory of ever reading picture books" (p. 120). I suspect Wilhelm's descriptions apply to most of Ann's poorer readers. If so, it is quite probable that working with others in book clubs helped these readers re-create the world of their stories.

The positive responses that students had to the literature are a credit to Ann. Many aspects of the unit contributed to their enjoyment of the literature. Participation in the selection and being able to read one of their top three choices certainly influenced the students' attitudes. And working in book clubs probably did, too. Enjoying multicultural literature was Ann's primary goal for her students, and she achieved her goal.

Readers' Future Literature Choices

In the Pre-Unit Survey, students were asked, "How do you usually feel about reading a new novel with characters who have different backgrounds and history from yours, and why [do you feel that way]?" After the unit, students were asked, "Would you choose to read another novel with characters who have a different background and history from yours in the future, and why or why not?" In statistical terms, the readers in this study didn't feel any differently after the unit (see Table 1). Approximately the same number of students who looked forward to reading about people different from themselves before they read their books indicated they would choose to read these types of books again. Before reading their novels, significantly more students felt positively (67.5%) than felt negatively (10.8%) about reading novels with characters who had different backgrounds and histories from their own. This did not change.

But there's an interesting story behind the numbers. Before beginning the unit, 56 of 83 students (67.5%) indicated that they usually had positive feelings about reading novels with characters who had different backgrounds and histories from their own. Forty-seven of these 56 students also turned in their Post-Unit Surveys. Of those 47, 37 said they would choose such a book again (7 said they would not, and 3 said they did not care either way). That is 80%, which is astonishing because, before beginning the unit, only 41% of the students who turned in the surveys (34 of 83) felt good about reading any kind of new novel. Looking at this another way, we see that prior to the unit, 41% of the readers who turned in surveys (34 of 83) felt good about reading new novels. After the unit, 54% (37 of 69) of all readers who turned in the surveys said

Table 1. Comparison of Responses

Pre-Unit Survey n = 83	How do you feel about reading a new novel with characters who have different backgrounds and histories than yours?	Post-Unit Survey n = 69	Would you read another novel with characters who have different backgrounds and histories from yours?
67.5%	Positive	72.5%	Yes
10.8%	Negative	14.5%	No
15.7%	Neutral	7.3%	Neutral
6.0%	Other	5.7%	Other

they would choose to read multicultural books again. Even if we assume that all the students who did not turn in the surveys decided they didn't want to read more multicultural books (quite unlikely), the percentage of students who would choose to read more still would have risen from 41% to 45% (37 of 83). This is an interesting finding, especially in light of the general feeling that students don't like to read multicultural literature.

The findings become even more interesting when we look at the seven readers (14.5%) who decided they would not choose such books again. The reasons they gave weren't at all what we've been led to expect. Of the seven, only two boys didn't want to read about people of different cultures. The other five didn't want to read any more about racism, or they disliked their books for reasons totally separate from their cultural components. The two boys who didn't want to read any more multicultural books had worked together in a book club. Two other readers, both girls, did not read the same book or work together and provided a stark contrast to the boys.

Before the unit, both Donald and Aaron were interested in learning about different cultures. Donald said, "I like it. It gives me a chance to learn more about different people I don't see on a day-to-day basis." Aaron said, "I usually feel like I want to learn more about the culture, I like to learn about things I don't know." As researcher, I don't know what happened, but by the time the boys had finished the unit, both had changed their minds. Donald said, "No [I wouldn't choose to read another book in which the characters had a different background and history from mine]. I like books about our own culture." And Aaron was just as clear: "No. I don't like to have to associate our culture with theirs. It's hard to learn."

On the other hand, the reasons Dawn and Allison gave for not choosing more multicultural books are strikingly different from the reasons the boys gave. Dawn, who read *Finding My Voice*, said she wouldn't choose to read another multicultural book because she "hate[s] hearing about racism." Allison read and liked *Shabanu* but worried about reading multicultural literature because she "might not know whether or not [the background and history] are true or a stereotype."

Reading about racism made one girl unhappy and one girl afraid she wouldn't recognize stereotypes when she read. Although these results are much too small to indicate a trend, they remind me of a study by Beverley Naidoo (1992). Using a racist perception scale she devised, Naidoo found "the existence of a clear gender pattern in response" (p. 31) among students in her study. She adds credibility to her findings by quoting the report of a project designed to reduce prejudice among primary school children in London: "Gender was…a highly significant variable in the pattern of response in both schools. Boys consistently displayed more overt and extreme forms of racism or ethnocentrism than girls…" (p. 145). As teachers, we need to look closely at the impact of male and female participation in literature circles and the impact of gender on responses to multicultural literature.

The remaining three readers who decided they would not choose to read another novel "whose characters have a different background and history from [theirs]," found their novels difficult to read. One reader thought her book took too long to get to the point and was thus confusing. Another student found *Morning Girl* "dull," so he said he wouldn't choose to read another multicultural book. The third student said, "Probably not. It's harder to understand."

Twenty-two other students turned in surveys after the unit. More than half (12 of 22) gave positive responses, indicating that they would choose to read more multicultural books.

Evidence of Aesthetic Transactions

The results discussed so far are a good indication that readers had aesthetic responses to the literature they read. But an aesthetic response involves more than just liking a book. It involves what Rosenblatt (1985) calls an aesthetic "trans-action" (p. 103). As described previously, during an aesthetic transaction, readers make for themselves their own unique creations of the text. By participating this way "in another's vision" (Rosenblatt, 1938/1976, p. 7), readers extend their understanding of what it means to be human. I wanted concrete evidence that Ann's readers participated in an aesthetic transaction.

I found the evidence in the Dialogue Journals. It was here that readers convinced the evaluators that they were participating in the stories. There was clear evidence that they were creating their own unique stories by experiencing "ideas, sensations, images, [and] tensions" (Rosenblatt, 1985, p. 103) they perceived in the text. Ann's actual written directions for the Dialogue Journals directed students to "select a character from the book and write about the story, events, yourself, and other characters from his/her point of view" (see Appendix B). Of the 75 students who turned in Dialogue Journals, all wrote under the names of characters. Of these 75, 93% were clearly operating within the story world. When Tonja became the character Shabanu, it was easy to recognize that she was enjoying a unique and pleasurable experience. She told her dialogue partner, "My family raises camels. Pretty soon we will be leaving for Sibi when we get there our camels will be loked at and some will be bought. I love taking care of the camels." Another student, Jason, seemed to be living in the story world, too, but his dialogue rang with angst and agony as he became Danny in *Shadow of the Dragon*:

> My family is just horrible. Ba, my gandmother, had a huge fight with Kim, my punkish sister. They were fighting because Kim was wearing really short skirts. I had to settle it since I'm the "anh-hai" or oldest son. Now Ba and Kim hate me.

I suspect that neither Tonja nor Jason understood the real dilemma of their respective characters, but that's not the issue here. Each had experienced "ideas, sensations, images, [and] tensions" in the process of giving birth to a story.

The five students in Ann's classes who did not operate within the story world responded quite differently. They acted either as a type of news reporter or went beyond the text to the extent that they appeared estranged from it. Tom, for example, after reading *Journey of the Sparrows*, played the role of reporter in this excerpt from his journal:

> I'm now half way through Chapter 2 and some new things have occured. Marias younger brother Oscar who has not eaten a lot and the next day Maria woke up. Oscar had been up all night and he would not talk or eat, but about

the only thing he would do was blink. Now Maria is in fear of losing her second brother the first came down with a bad case of worms and now Maria is in fear of losing Oscar to the same awful and painful disease and later maybe death.

When John, on the other hand, wrote as Tomper from *Finding My Voice*, he reported events and focused on material not contained in the text at all. He began his first entry,

My name is Tomper Sondel. I play football and hockey. I am a handsome chap. I could basically get any girl in my school but I like only Ellen Sung.... There is this other girl who I started to like also.... She is the prettiest girl in our school. I don't know which to choose.

When his dialogue partner responded from a closer reading of text, "No offense, but you sound pretty arrogant and over-confident in yourself," John, as Tomper, replied, "I am not overconfident. I know for a fact that I am the handsomest guy in the school. My hair color is blond. I am just as normal as you except I get all of the woman and you don't." After this exchange, John continued his dialogue but changed the subject, claiming he didn't care about either of the girls, and began talking about microwave hamburgers, Star Wars videos, and Brady Bunch movies.

The kind of enthusiasm for multicultural literature exhibited by Ann's readers is exciting and encouraging because the findings differ from those of an important study conducted from 1991 to 1995 by faculty and graduate students at the National Center for Research in the Learning and Teaching of Literature at the University at Albany, State University of New York, USA. The study revealed that students were much more concerned with "survival in school reading" (Cruz et al., 1997, p. 5) than they were with reading or learning about cultures other than their own. An interesting aspect of the study was that, according to Purves (project leader for the study), most of the teachers interviewed held what he called a bazaar or inclusionist view of multiculturalism. Teachers who favor this approach tend to see the United States as a melting pot, ignoring the different or distinct features of cultures in favor of focusing on their similarities, often presuming a false sense of unity. That is very different from Ann's perspective, which is that cultures are unique and that only by recognizing and celebrating their distinct features can the United States reach its full potential. Although neither study was designed to measure the relationship between teachers' views of multiculturalism and the outcomes of students' reading, the contrast is interesting.

Aesthetic Response and Social Responsibility

Politics and literature seem like strange bedfellows to many teachers. Perhaps that is because we were taught to think that way. Dan Hade (1997), author of many articles about children's literature and social justice and a former editor of *The New Advocate*, insists that many of us have been taught the myth that

> stories have no political meaning or that to make a political meaning will over-power the aesthetic value of literature. We were taught and we continue to teach in our schools that, under the laws of the United States, race, class, and gender do not matter; we are equal. (p. 251)

Although stories may be political, it is readers who make political meaning, and the meaning readers make is a part of their aesthetic responses.

Naidoo (1992) grew up white and middle class in South Africa during the period of apartheid. She writes of becoming intensely angry at the narrowness of her schooling and at "its complicity in perpetuating apartheid through not previously challenging my blinkered vision" (p. 9). Naidoo eventually moved to England and wrote several young adult novels reflecting the consequences of apartheid in her home country, where those novels were banned. She also wrote *Through Whose Eyes? Exploring Racism: Reader, Text, and Context* (1992), an outgrowth of her doctoral research. In explaining why she decided to conduct research in a predominantly white area, Naidoo quotes the Commission for Racial Equality (1988) when she writes that "the perpetuators of racist abuse within schools are not a lunatic fringe but 'ordinary, everyday members of the learning community' spanning students, staff, and parents" (p. 15), and she quotes Stuart Hall (1985) as pointing out that racism is as much "a structured absence, a not speaking about things, as it is a positive setting up of attitudes to race" (p. 15).

Writing about the relationship between reading and prejudice, Sara Zimet (1976) says,

> Both personal testimony and empirical research strongly suggest that while our attitudes, values, and behaviours may be influenced by what we read, when left to our own initiative *we read what we are*. In other words, we select our reading to support our predispositions rather than in order to change them. (p. 17)

Beginning with this quote, Naidoo goes on to argue, as Zimet does, that the context in which reading is done can have an impact on attitudes, values, and behaviors. She argues that teachers and teaching are important because they can influence readers and, when readers change, they change the texts they read.

Many U.S. classroom teachers are struggling against heavy odds to change situations like those in which Naidoo found herself as a child. Ann is one of those teachers. In his study, Ostrowski (1997) focused on 25 secondary teachers from across the United States who regularly used multicultural literature in their classrooms. He refutes the challenges of critics who contend that teachers are sacrificing literary quality for inclusion or that teachers are using literature "as a tool for shaping or changing society rather than as a primarily aesthetic object that, if it shapes or changes society, does so with some degree of subtlety" (p. 54). Instead, he found that "teachers care very deeply that the works they choose possess literary merit...that they are indeed aesthetic objects, and that not any work...will suffice" (p. 54). In light of Ostrowski's research, Ann's efforts may be a prototype of the efforts of many teachers. He says that teachers

> are forced in the course of their typically heavy daily schedules to search for, buy (often with their own money), read, and try to determine the appropriateness of various works of literature from different cultures and sometimes different historical periods. (p. 55)

Similar to Ann, the teachers in Ostrowski's study were not comfortable with a single piece of literature being used to "represent" a culture and

> they were often unsure if a work they were using or considering would accurately portray life in a given culture. They weren't always certain if the actions of important characters were typical or atypical of persons in a given cultural context. (p. 55)

The teachers also were faced with concerns about providing equal time for all cultures, creating new curricula, and learning about the authors and the cultural and historical backgrounds of the literature. Finally, the teachers often had reservations about their own abilities to teach multicultural literature. In her teaching, Ann faced all these concerns either implicitly or explicitly.

The Impact of Culture

Taking a step back, we know that the readers in Ann's classes did read and respond to the stories they read, and they did participate in aesthetic transactions. Altieri (1996) describes a related finding when she read stories aloud to fifth and seventh graders that reflected cultural groups different from the culture of the listeners. Altieri found that the students' written responses after hearing the stories indicated that "overall, the level of aesthetic involvement was not significantly influenced by the ethnicity of student or culture portrayed in the story" (p. 237). Studies like Altieri's indicate that neither the culture of the author nor the culture of the reader interferes with *aesthetic* response. However, other studies show that what students learn from their culture does influence their *understanding* of what they read (e.g., Heath, 1983; Reynolds, Taylor, Steffensen, Shirey, & Anderson, 1982; Steffensen, Joag-Dev, & Anderson, 1979). Findings of researchers such as Heath, Reynolds, and Steffensen are particularly relevant to the findings discussed in this chapter because most of Ann's students came from a culture that was strongly homogeneous. The students belonged to a community of white, middle- and working-class families. Less than 10% of the students in the school came from ethnic backgrounds of color. That their culture had a strong impact on them is reinforced further by students' self-identification on their Post-Unit Surveys that members of their families, together with the media, were the primary sources of what they knew about cultures other than their own.

Steffensen and her colleagues (1979) conducted a unique and often-quoted research study about the powerful impact of culture. They designed a brief, limited, controlled experiment from which they determined that a reader's cultural knowledge and beliefs influence what the reader comprehends from a text. Reynolds and his colleagues (1982) took Steffensen's work a step further, attempting to determine whether "despite the large amount of cultural overlap, differences of sufficient magnitude exist among groups in the United States to have an important influence on text interpretations" (p. 357). They studied the responses of 105 eighth graders—54 from a black, working-class area and 51 from a white, agricultural area—in Tennessee and two towns in Illinois. Approximately half were boys and half were girls. The students read a letter purporting to be about a school incident. It was possible to interpret the letter as reporting a fight or describing an incident involving "sounding" or "playing the dozens," a form of ritual verbal insult common among black adolescent males. The white students tended to interpret the letter as being about a fight, but the black students, familiar with sounding, interpreted the letter as an instance of that event. Based on their results, Reynolds and his colleagues concluded that "cultural schemata can influence how prose material is interpreted" (p. 353).

In 1983, Shirley Brice Heath published what has become a classic study testifying to the impact of culture on children. *Ways With Words* is an ethnographic account of almost 10 years she spent interacting with three different communities. Heath describes the dramatic interaction between home socialization and schooling. She documents the differences in the ways communities socialize their children, and she demonstrates the dramatic impact of that socialization on children's performance in school. Heath also describes the implications of that socialization for the children, their communities, and society in general.

Research demonstrates that culture permeates all responses to literature, even those that appear to be the most personal. For example, Mauro (1984) studied readers' oral responses to selected literature about death and dying. She found that they responded using three different sets of constructs, or understandings: a construct for the specific content of the story; a construct for literary characteristics, or form, through which they viewed the texts; and a construct for process, a personal way of reading and responding to a text that was a combination of developmental abilities related to response, school training, and past experiences in responding to literature. Although some of the constructs were more permeable than others for particular readers, Mauro concluded that "all four of these readers [had] sets of personal constructs related to content, form, and process...[and that] differences in basic construct systems result in different constructions of texts" (p. 171). Even constructs about death, although personal and individual, are culturally situated.

Another researcher, Wason-Ellam (1997), collected ethnographic data in an inner-city school over a two-year period. She found that the 8-year-old girls in her study, who were from working-class communities, most often made links to "physically attractive and youthful personas in televised 'soaps' and MTV videos" (p. 434). Wason-Ellam notes, "talk about being feminine often regulate[d] subculture, class identity, and power" (p. 434). She concluded that

> stories are informed by a group's cultural ways.... Through the continual layering and intertextuality of such stories and their visual images, the focal girls constructed their own knowledge by acting within a social context that shapes and constrains that knowledge. In this way, they learn the gendered ways to participate in a culture. (p. 435)

As a result of her findings, Wason-Ellam writes that "children's readings, based on their own cultural and social experiences, may be quite different from their teachers', leading students to *read* progressive texts in less-than-progressive ways" (p. 436).

Unlike readers in Ann's classes who had little or no experience with any literature, let alone multicultural literature, the girls in Wason-Ellam's study were regularly involved in a quality literature curriculum. If the long-standing assumptions about the influence of literature on readers are accurate, we would expect the girls in Wason-Ellam's study to be affected by what they had read. However, Wason-Ellam states that the girls had established ideas about appropriate gender behavior and were "often unwilling to deviate from their values and beliefs" (p. 436). She further argues that "young readers don't merely absorb the values of a story, even if these values are progressive...and of ultimate advantage to them" (p. 436).

Assumptions About "Otherness"

As mentioned earlier, Ann's journal notes revealed that she was involved in a difficult professional struggle. Although she felt a strong professional need to challenge her students to think more deeply about the literature, she was aware of the strong reader response movement in the United States, and she was aware that she needed to support readers' personal responses. Although Ann's primary goal was for students to enjoy reading and understanding novels, her assignments varied in the stance they encouraged; for example, the Book Club Organizer encouraged a much more efferent stance than the Dialogue Journal did. Overall, however, the multicultural literature unit was quite different from the others taught during the year, particularly because students were given significant responsibility for interpretation. In other words, students played a much larger role in responding to and understanding their books while Ann played a much smaller role. Throughout the unit, students appeared to enjoy responding in ways that involved personal response. However, they also created responses that reflected the shared or cultural significance their book clubs found in the works. In fact, the book club project was the assignment they enjoyed the most and from which they felt they learned the most. It also may have been the one most influenced by the culture of their community.

At the beginning of this section, I wrote that readers make political meaning and that the meaning they make is part of their aesthetic responses. A pivotal finding that emerged from the students' responses was so obvious that I had never even considered it; however, it is a crucial finding if we want to understand our students' responses to multicultural literature. For most of Ann's students, being American meant being part of the "in-group." And, for these students, the in-group is white. What Ann's students didn't realize was that people from nondominant cultural groups were, in fact, American citizens. The students did not perceive African Americans, Latina/Latino Americans, Asian

Americans, or Native Americans to be American in the same way they saw themselves as Americans. Instead, they perceived anyone who looked different as being a foreigner—either literally or figuratively—an assumption that revealed a strong underlying us-versus-them mentality. I cannot imagine a more political reading.

The written work of 57 students in Ann's classes provided indirect evidence that 88% of the students did not recognize that Korean Americans, Vietnamese Americans, or Chinese Americans were U.S. citizens; only 12% did. (The papers of 57 students were used here because it was not possible to reliably determine the assumptions of the other 26.) If these percentages are accurate, that would mean that of 100 readers who read about a Korean American, such as Ellen in *Finding My Voice*, 88 readers would *assume* they were reading about a person from Korea rather than about another U.S. citizen.

Although students did not assume that African Americans and Latina/Latino Americans were from a different country, the us-versus-them mentality was clearly present in their written responses, with "us" being white and the norm for what it means to be an "American." The implications and ramifications of this kind of thinking are enormous, especially in light of the September 11, 2001, terrorist attacks and the potential consequences for anyone who does not look white.

Even the seven students who did recognize that, for instance, *Koreans* and *Korean Americans* were different often used these labels inconsistently, indicating that they, too, vacillated in their understanding of citizen and noncitizen. It is important to note that more than half the students who recognized that people commonly identified with a dual label (e.g., Korean Americans) were U.S. citizens and not foreigners were themselves children of nondominant cultures. Consider Gil, for example, who identified himself as Chinese American and, in his responses, clearly recognized the duality children from nondominant groups often experience in their lives and reflected on the struggles they have. He reflected on the conflict faced by many second-generation Asian Americans of finding a balance between traditional Asian and contemporary American lifestyle when he said, "My parents try to make a lot of decision for me. But I keep saying I have to make decision for my self." In another response, he used the appropriate designator when he explained, "I used to have a lot of African American friends. A lot of them are easy to get along with." Yet when he explained what positive things he knew or believed about people who are Korean Americans, Gil appeared to equate Korean Americans with Korean nationals saying, "Koreans developed Tae Kwan Do."

It is tempting to dismiss this by saying it doesn't matter, that Gil meant *Korean American*, or that Gil surely knows the difference. Yet other responses indicated that Gil clearly thought of people of nondominant groups as "other." For example, he wrote that "a lot of [Vietnamese Americans] live in the ghetto"; people from Pakistan "have aranged marages"; and Latina/Latino Americans "give you cheap labor." Even though he is a U.S. citizen, perhaps Gil feels himself to be on the outside because he looks "Chinese" rather than "American," as the dominant culture perceives American.

Jody's entries appear to reflect an understanding that the author of *Finding My Voice*, like the main character, struggled with the effects of racism, yet Jody uses *Korean* and *Korean American* interchangeably. In one place, she wrote, "The woman who wrote the book is of the Korean-American nationality," yet in another place she noted, "The author is Korean and she wrote about Korean people. She knows what it's like because she lived through it." Because it's clear that Jody doesn't recognize the significance of the label, it's important to question whether she understands that living through it as a citizen means more than coming to grips with being different—it is being denied your rights as a U.S. citizen.

Even when students did seem to recognize an American component of a dual identity, their knowledge and understanding was not only limited but also inaccurate. For example, Kathy wrote, "Probably the only thing I know about Korean Americans is that they are from Korea," but what she knows is simply inaccurate. Many Korean Americans, although their ancestors are from Korea, have never even been to Korea. They were born in the United States, and their families may have been U.S. citizens longer than Kathy's family has. But at least Kathy reflected on what she thought she knew and tried to be accountable for her assumptions:

> I don't know many things about the Chinese Americans. I can only go [by] what I see. Chinese people have small eyes, but I haven't seen every person, so I don't know if they all have small eyes. I'm sorry to say, but I don't know hardly anything about Latino Americans, than their spanish. They come from Cuba. Even this information is probably wrong.

Kathy is right about one thing: She is wrong.

Although occasionally a student gave clear evidence of recognizing the American component of a dual identity, this rarely occurred. One example appeared in Syd's Dialogue Journal. While writing in his Dialogue Journal as Danny, the main character in *Shadow of the Dragon*, Syd referred to himself as

Vietnamese but said of his mom, "She made a mistake at the thingie to become an Amiricn type of person." It is obvious that Syd recognized that Vietnamese and Vietnamese American are different. He even highlighted it.

As previously mentioned, in the study conducted by the National Center for Research in the Learning and Teaching of Literature (Cruz et al.,1997), Purves and his colleagues found that most teachers in the study held an inclusionist view of multiculturalism. That is, they preferred to ignore the different or distinct features of cultures in favor of focusing on people as alike. Perhaps the teachers were merely trying to counteract what they perceived as their students' attitudes that people with dual identifiers were different. On the other hand, it may be that the teachers themselves perceived people from nondominant cultures to be different (it may even be that the teachers assumed people of other ethnicities to be immigrants and, thus, not really U.S. citizens). And because the majority of teachers are white (National Center for Education Statistics, 1997), they can then play the role of defender, denying obvious differences and insisting that what is different, both in appearance and in power, is alike.

Challenging the Status Quo

Ann does not ascribe to an inclusionist view of multiculturalism, nor does she ignore differences between cultures. Instead, including multicultural literature in her curriculum was a way of celebrating those differences and of calling attention to the unearned advantage some groups of people have. Yet after her unit, 88% of her students still saw people in the United States who were not white as foreigners. It is clear that teachers need to clarify and challenge students' understanding of what it means to be a U.S. citizen. All citizens are equal under the law—none are more equal than others—regardless of heritage. It may be worthwhile to point out the terrible consequences in the United States when this was misunderstood, such as the Jim Crow laws, women being denied the right to vote, the Japanese American internment, and the ongoing controversy about making English the official language of the United States and the related issue of limiting bilingual education.

This finding highlights another separate but related issue: Teachers need to challenge students' perceptions that the roots of dominant-culture people are "American," but the roots of people from nondominant cultures are "foreign." Even my white college students see their roots as being in the United States, not Europe. This reinforces their perception of themselves as "American" and nondominant peoples as the "other." For example, my European American students think their folk tales originated in the United States. They don't realize that many of their folk tales are from Northern and Western Europe just as the folk tales of Latina/Latino Americans and Vietnamese Americans are from their ancestral homes. Some students think they've been in the United States longer. They don't realize that many Mexican Americans have always lived here and have been "American" since their homeland became part of the United States when the Treaty of Guadalupe Hidalgo was signed in 1848. Some European American students don't realize that many Asian Americans have been here for five, six, or seven generations—far longer than many of their own families have.

There are several very practical ways of addressing the issue of us versus them, citizen versus noncitizen. One way is to separate literature about citizens from literature about internationals. In Ann's unit, there was no such division. In fact, the distinctions were often blurred and might have easily reinforced the assumption that all characters, other than those from the dominant culture, are "other." The main characters in two of the books, *Finding My Voice* and *Scorpions*, are U.S. citizens who are Korean American and African American, respectively. Danny's citizenship status in *Shadow of the Dragon* is not explicitly defined, but early in the book Danny defines himself in contrast to his immigrant cousin when he says, "I am an American." Although born in Vietnam, Danny and his parents have lived in the United States for at least 10 years and see the country as their home, even helping other family members to immigrate to the United States. The contrast between a U.S. citizen and a non–U.S. citizen is further reinforced by Danny's newly arrived cousin from Vietnam. In *Scorpions*, the two main characters—Jamal and Tito—are both U.S. citizens, but at the end of the book Tito is sent to Puerto Rico (seen by most readers as a foreign place) with his grandmother. *Morning Girl* is a historical fiction story set in 1642. Although the Taino Indians were some of the earliest known inhabitants of North America, the historical nature of the story creates the impression that they are quite foreign to current U.S. culture. *Journey of the Sparrows* is about illegal immigrants who live in Chicago, Illinois. Although the characters live in the United States and engender much sympathy, they are clearly not "Americans." *Waiting for the Rain* and *Shabanu* are set in South Africa and Pakistan, respectively, and their characters are residents of those countries. However, in *Waiting for the Rain*, one character is white and one is black (I will talk later about the importance of this to readers in Ann's class). Because no distinction was made between the citizen-versus-noncitizen status of the characters and because this was a unit about "other" cultures, it was easy for students to see the characters in all the books as "different" and, by implication, "not American."

Another practical suggestion is to make a clear distinction between literature about immigration and literature about long-term residents. Immigration literature has a number of distinct characteristics. Because characters in these books are recent immigrants, they face unusual difficulties. On one hand, they must acclimate to such things as different customs, cultural norms, and language patterns. Older immigrants, including parents of the child characters, often make great efforts to assimilate into the mainstream culture while simultaneously struggling to maintain the culture of their homeland. They often fear their children are losing the "old" ways. The child characters, on the other hand, frequently feel trapped between two worlds, desperately wishing to be "American" in every sense of the word while living with parents who maintain traditional practices and adhere to traditional norms. While many dominant culture readers respond positively to this strong desire of nondominant characters to assimilate, to "fit in," to be "American," most people of nondominant cultures are not immigrants but citizens. Immigration literature is important, but so is literature that presents characters as citizens who are confident in their identities, are integral members of society, and are not seeking the approval from Euro-American society.

It is also important to recognize that reading one multicultural book is not enough. In this study it appeared that for many readers one story became representative of a whole culture because it was the only book of its kind that students had read. Reading only one book may result in reinforcing or introducing significant misunderstandings and stereotypes. As teachers, we need to find a way to overcome the limitations imposed by using one text when students have limited exposure to the experiences of different cultural groups. No one book or author can be held responsible for reflecting the entire experience of a group of people. If a reader reads only one book reflecting the experiences of a cultural group, that book is likely to have a strong impact on that reader's perception of the cultural group even if he or she is later exposed to different perspectives. It even may reinforce existing stereotypes or introduce new ones. Teacher book talks and reading lists that suggest titles of multicultural literature as options for additional required reading would be helpful in extending readers' experiences. Exposure to other books, movies, videos, documentaries, poems, songs, interviews, and one-on-one interaction with people of the culture are all ways in which readers can enrich their understandings of a culture.

It is particularly interesting that, in this study, all students—those who liked to read and those who did not like to read—enjoyed the multicultural novels. There is little doubt that they liked the multicultural books they read or that they participated in aesthetic transactions with the literature they read. However, what students learned about their own culture and the cultures of others has far-reaching implications for teaching.

Does all this mean that using multicultural literature in the classroom is a worthless activity? Far from it. It does mean that we need to consider the influence of the cultural groups to which readers belong (e.g., the culture, the family, the literature group, and the literature read because literature is filtered through the lens of these identities). Remember, Ann's readers had exposure to literature and media that were strongly tied to and reflective of the dominant white culture in U.S. society. If cultures are, by definition, exclusionary and people of one culture see people of other cultures as "outside, above, or beneath them" (Jordan & Purves, 1993, p. 1), being part of the dominant culture means being part of the in-group. All of us obtain our identities from the cultural groups to which we belong. As children develop their concepts of self, the groups to which they belong—the culture, the family, the peer group—exert powerful influence (Allport, 1954/1958; Beach & Freedman, 1992; Heath, 1983). The Pre-Unit Survey completed by Ann's students indicated that they had strongly stereotyped views of nondominant cultures. This had direct implications for the students' book clubs in which the shared cultural significance they created took on a unique cast. In chapter 3, I look at how that played out in the students' written responses and at what other researchers have found in their studies, because the answers might provide a road map for you in your own classroom.

Learning About Cultures

[The projects] were dull; some were disrespectful to the cultural group they represented. [One] group—of very bright girls—did [their entire project] on arranged marriages—they missed everything else in Shabanu. *How could I have missed the boat with them so completely? It just seems like no matter how hard I work, nothing real and tangible gets accomplished. (Ann)*

Ann made this comment in her journal near the end of the unit. It is obvious that she was discouraged. Did she miss the boat? Did she accomplish anything? Did she fail? In this chapter, I consider what the students learned from the multicultural literature they read. What did they learn about cultures different from their own? Did their respect for their own culture and cultural heritage increase? Did their respect for the culture and cultural heritage of other people increase? Did their cross-cultural understanding increase? Did it free them from "the bondage of stereotypes" (Cai, 1997, p. 210)? What can we learn from what happened in Ann's classroom, and what might that mean for you and your students?

To evaluate how effective the unit was, I had to determine the extent to which Ann's students achieved the culture-related objectives she had set for the unit. The first objective was that students learn about the norms and values of cultures different from their own. The second objective was that students increase their understanding of themselves and their own culture. To achieve these objectives, Ann realized that she would need to encourage and support readers in questioning both the content of the books they read and the authors' presentation of that content. Ann also wanted her students to recognize the impact of being a member of a nondominant culture in the United States. She wanted them to recognize that characters of nondominant cultures in the books they read thought, spoke, acted, and reacted using the norms and values of their own cultures, but she also wanted her students to recognize diversity within cultural groups. In all this, she wanted her readers to see people from nondominant cultures as whole people with a full range of human experiences, not as victims. Did she achieve her goal? The answer is both yes and no. What students learned about their own culture and the cultures of others and the meanings that students created in their book clubs took on a unique cast.

Recognizing Worldview

To help determine whether Ann's students had met the first goal, I wanted to find out if students recognized that the primary characters in their books think, act, and react with a worldview—in most cases different from that of the reader—which affects their decisions, actions, and reactions. To answer this question, evaluators looked at three assignments: the Book Club Organizer, the Dialogue Journal, and the Post-Unit Survey. Recognizing a character's worldview as different from one's own means recognizing that a character's actions evolve from a unique set of values and beliefs, often different from the readers' values and beliefs. It means recognizing that even though the character's way of acting seems similar to that of the reader, the reasons for those actions are different. It also involves the recognition that people of a particular culture share a common way of seeing the world. An example might be the way Danny acts in *Shadow of the Dragon*. Early in the story, he rescues two girls from several aggressive members of the Cobra gang. A reader from the dominant culture might see this action as brave or heroic, whereas members of the culture reflected in the book might see it as Danny's duty because he is an older male.

In chapter 1, I talked about the stances readers adopt when reading. In this case, it did not appear to make any difference whether readers were involved in traditional, school-type assignments, such as the Book Club Organizer that focused on obtaining information, or whether they were involved in assignments that involved them in aesthetic experiences during which they participated in "virtual" experiences in a new world. Readers responding to both assignments appeared to recognize that characters from nondominant cultures operate with a unique worldview that affects their decisions, actions, and reactions. Three quarters of readers on both assignments (76% and 73%, respectively) did appear to recognize that the character from the nondominant culture operates from a different set of underlying cultural assumptions; one quarter did not. However, these percentages reversed on the Post-Unit Survey when students were asked about people rather than characters in literature. Less than 25% appeared to recognize that people from non-dominant cultures operate from different underlying cultural assumptions. The rest gave no evidence that they recognized this.

Providing examples that demonstrate students' recognition of different worldviews and their implications is difficult because decisions were based on an entire assignment, not just a sentence or two. But, the following examples might help.

Aaron and Robert were in the same class and both read *Shadow of the Dragon*. Because they read the same book, Aaron and Robert were in the same book club and worked together on their Book Club Organizers. Both boys noted the influence of family in the main character's decisions. Aaron explained that Danny tries to keep Sang Le and Kim out of trouble because of his commitment to his family, and Robert noted that Danny tries to keep Sang Le as a friend because of his commitment to family, and Danny tells police about [the attack on Sang Le] because he felt he "owed" Sang Le. An understanding of Danny's unique worldview also appeared in both boys' Dialogue Journals. Pretending to be Danny, Aaron wrote to a partner who read *Finding My Voice*, "I sometimes don't like being this old. I have to settle arguments around our house because Mom and Dad shouldn't be disturbed with things we argue about. This joy always falls on the oldest son." Robert corresponded with a journal partner who had read *Scorpions*. When his partner asked Robert, as Danny, why his grandmother, Ba, hates anything American, Robert replied, "I think it's because she thinks it's fake and she really respects Vietnamese culture and won't go American."

However, although both Aaron and Robert reflected in their Book Club Organizers and Dialogue Journals an understanding that Danny operates with a unique worldview, Aaron continued to reflect this understanding in his Post-Unit Survey, but Robert did not. Each responded quite differently. When asked what he knew about people who are Vietnamese American, Aaron continued to demonstrate his understanding of specific norms and values when he wrote, "Vietnamese Americans are smart, close to the rest of family, and sacrifice for each other. They are discriminated against, thought to be in gangs [and to] not have advanced cities (farm)." Conversely, Robert appeared not to remember what he reflected on earlier about Vietnamese heritage and its impact on Danny's thinking and his actions. He replied simply with the stereotypical generalization that Vietnamese Americans are "good actors and involved in gangs."

Jason, a second-generation Chinese American, provided another interesting example, using his own experience to help him understand the effect of culture on the family dynamics in *Shadow of the Dragon*. In his Book Club Organizer, he explained,

> I think Danny's family and world are pretty similar to mine. My grandma is like Ba. Both value luck and old traditions and customs. My world is also troubled, many bad things happen to me too. My family values their oldest son, me, because I will carry on their last name.

However, by the time Jason completed his Post-Unit Survey, he reverted to generalizations and stereotypes—even though they were generally positive—showing little connection to the insight he demonstrated earlier about the characters. Almost 80% of the readers appeared, as Jason did, to make a clean break between characters in literature and people in real life. Jason said he

> knows that many [Chinese Americans] are great figure skaters or authors, that many [African Americans] are very talented in sports, and that some [Vietnamese Americans] are very accomplished people and lead wonderful lives.

Given this tendency to generalize or stereotype, it is not surprising that, somewhere in their writing, 80% of the readers consciously or unconsciously noted stereotypical characteristics of different cultural groups, such as skin color or typical food preferences. For example, students might have referred to Chinese Americans as short in stature or good cooks or to African Americans as good athletes. Nathan did this when asked what positive things he knew or believed about Chinese Americans. He said that Chinese Americans are "good cooks, tend to be artistic, and are usually intelligent." Nathan learned this "eat[ing] at numerous Chinese restaurants and see[ing] delicate artwork on their walls." He said he also knew "that they do well in college" because he hears this on the news. When asked what negative things he knew about Chinese Americans, it was clear that Nathan was referring not to reality but to a learned stereotype. Although he may have been referring to Chinese Americans, it is more likely that he was referring to his perception of a stereotypical Chinatown—or even to a hypothetical Asian country—when he said they "tend to live in dirty, sleazy, pornographic towns. Sex is common."

Assuming a Character's Perspective

Next, each evaluator read the students' Dialogue Journals to determine if the students appeared to understand what it meant to be African American or

Korean American in the United States, to be black in South Africa, or to be Islamic and female in the Cholistan Desert of Pakistan. When students wrote from the perspectives of chosen characters, were they able to become the characters? Were they able to express what it is like to be part of a cultural group with unique customs, characteristics, and language patterns that inevitably result in what Sims (1982) calls a unique "worldview or culture or sensibility" (p. 13)? Did they recognize when being part of a nondominant-cultural group resulted, for their character, in internal struggles between two worlds?

Characters often struggle with conflicts between their peer groups and the expectations of their parents. But in multicultural literature, characters struggle with an additional conflict: They must cope simultaneously with two sets of conflicting expectations. For example, Ellen, the main character in *Finding My Voice*, is faced with two conflicting sets of cultural values: the Korean values held by her immigrant parents and the dominant-culture values held by her friends and their parents. Because readers in this study were almost exclusively white and, therefore, part of the dominant culture, it was important to determine if they recognized such internal struggles and that they were related to ethnicity. Because characters of nondominant cultures are often portrayed as less affluent than dominant-culture characters, such struggles can be easily misunderstood as issues of socioeconomic class rather than accurately understood as conflicts resulting from different norms and values. For example, being in a gang is not a result of ethnicity, but the way a family reacts to a young person being in a gang may be, as is the case with Jamal's family in *Scorpions*. In the same way, Danny's need to be home for the Vietnamese New Year's in *Shadow of the Dragon* is directly related to the values and norms of his Vietnamese family. Children of other groups may need to be home for New Year's, too, but in this book the situation is directly related to Danny's cultural background.

Two thirds of Ann's students (p < .002) were able to become the characters and to feel what it was like to be part of a group with a unique worldview that involved customs, characteristics, and language patterns. They appeared to understand, either implicitly or explicitly, that the characters' struggles, motivations, or actions evolve from a unique set of values and beliefs—values and beliefs shared by members of the cultural group but different from those of the reader. Even though the actions of a character often seemed similar to the way the reader might act, the reader recognized, to some extent, that the reasons for those actions were different. For example, in *Morning Girl*, Star Boy becomes a rock. A naive reader from the dominant culture might think Star

Boy is pretending to hide or playing hide-and-seek. For many Native Americans, however, Star Boy's actions capture the intimate relationship between human beings and the natural world. The following excerpts from students' Dialogue Journals demonstrate the difference between the writing of students who understood the effect of a specific cultural worldview and those who did not. Julie, for example, recognized the fears and struggles of not only being an illegal immigrant but also of being a Hispanic illegal immigrant who is also part of family with its own unique values. Jim, on the other hand, did not reveal the same understanding in his description.

Feb. 14

Dear Sissy,

Hello. My name is Maria. I am in Chicago, Illinois. I am an illegal alien from El Salvador. I am 15 years old. I came to America with my sister, Julia, who is pregnant, my younger brother Oscar, and another boy, Tomas. The conditions in the crate were terrible—no food or water. Oscar would "wet himself" in the crate and I was shoved up against Tomas' body—what would mother and grandmother think if they knew? There were some very scary men at the places where we stopped and got out. We also heard many cries from other crates. When our journey was over, Tomas's aunt, Marta, picked us up and brought us to her home.

Sincerely, Maria [alias Julie]

Feb. 14

Dear Jason,

Hi My name is Tomas and I am an immigrant I am traveling in a crate on my way to Chicago I am traviling with a girl names Julia and her sister Maria and there little brother Oscar. He just wet all over Maria leg. I am standing very close to Julia.

Tomas [alias Jim]

Like Julie, Sally and Paula were able to see through the eyes of their respective characters, reflecting struggles, motivations, or actions of their characters that resulted from being members of nondominant cultures. Sally, writing as Jamal in *Scorpions*, captured Jamal's strong attachment to and concern for his family as he tries to help his brother by maintaining his own credibility with the gang, and at the same time he tries not to hurt their mother:

My Mama is trying to make enough cash to live on. But it is tough. We live in an apartment with two small bedrooms. But I sleep on the couch.... I don't want to follow in Randy's footsteps but I might have to.... My Mom is very sad about

Randy.... I have a gun and held it on Dwayne. He told the police so now I am in deep shi* [*sic*] too. I don't want to hurt Mama though.

Paula read *Shabanu*, a novel in which the main character has to marry against her wishes because she is female and her nomadic family needs access to land with water. Even though she would have been happier marrying a younger man, Shabanu's struggle goes beyond the issue of marriage to address the role of women in her society. Assuming the identity of Phulan, Shabanu's older sister, Paula reflected Phulan's acceptance of her own role as well as Shabanu's resistance:

> Then after Rahim, Nazir Mohammad's brother, tried to get Nazir to not take Murad's land if Shabanu would marry him, Mami and Dadi agreed so Shabanu shall marry Rahim a 50-year old who is very wealthy and she will be his fourth wife. I married Murad. We live in a beautiful home and we are praying that we will be blessed with sons. Our wedding ceremony was very nice and I am proud to be Murad's wife. Shabanu, my sister is 13 years old and she is very smart. I feel bad that she must marry Rahim because I know she would rather stay as a desert girl. We are quite different because she is much more loud and unhappy.

Barbara read *Shabanu*, too. However, although she recognized the predicament of the main character, unlike Paula, her cavalier tone does not reflect Shabanu's struggles, either with the demands placed on her by her culture or with her own personal abhorrence of having to marry Rahim:

> Dear Mary,
> Hi! Today I found out that I am being forced to marry Rahim. I don't really like it but I don't have a say i the matter either. Also, when I was 11 years old, he was 55! That's a big range! Plus, I don't want to marry someone that much older then me but it's part of our culture that has gone on for a long time so I guess I can't break it now! Who know, maybe I'll end up liking him! Just look at Phulan, she likes Murad and it was planned! I'll just go through with it. Well, I'm gonna go now. I'll write later!
> Shabanu [alias Barbara]

In a similar way, Ellen's matter-of-fact retelling of episodes in Jamal's life belies her failure to understand the emotional struggle facing Jamal when his opportunity to help his family by joining the gang conflicts with his mother's wishes:

> Debbie,
> Well, how are you doing. Me well I've been into lots of fights and Mack gave me a gun so I'm getting into a lot of trouble with that and Tito my friend got

cought with it and got kick out at the park I got into the gange and was the leader. I had a job but the members of the gange ruined it for me will I tried to quit the gange that didn't work out to well Indian and Angel jumped me and almost killed me Tito shot both of them and he told the police and he had to move back to Peurto Rico with his father. My brother got stabbed in jail but he is better and for me I quit the gange and Mack stood up for me but that's the end so I better go know.

Sincerly,

Jamal Hicks [alias Ellen]

Although two thirds of Ann's students reflected the impact of ethnicity when writing in their Dialogue Journals, 25% wrote entries that were more reflective of the reader's personality than that of the character. Rather than perceiving the influence ethnicity has on their characters, they wrote from their own perspectives, even though they used the names of the characters. For example, in the following entry, although Nick assumed the voice of Jamal, his entry reflected an arrogance that appeared throughout his written assignments, but which is not characteristic of Jamal:

> My friend is Tito he is a cool kid man. I want to be the bad guy because my brother is and I think that I have to be just like him. I don't know why but I don't wuss out. My friend wants to be in the Scorpions because there the best and he wants to be the best.

Similar to Nick, Cheryl incorporated material that may reflect her own worldview but that is uncharacteristic of the Asian American character, Ellen. Not only did she attribute a resignation to Ellen that doesn't appear in the book, but, in doing so, she missed Ellen's intense feelings about school, relationships, and family:

> I think I'm going out for gymnastics because Beth is too.... Beth is just one of my normal hang out with friends and we do stuff on occasions.... I have some really good news. I got in to Harvard but the bas news is because of it I'm broken up with Tomper. Well out of something good I guess there's always something bad.

It was interesting that more than 12% of readers who turned in the Dialogue Journals chose to assume the role of the dominant-culture characters in their stories even though the characters from the nondominant culture were clearly the main characters. All had read either *Waiting for the Rain* or *Finding My Voice* and wrote as Frikke or Tromper, respectively. These books were the only two in the unit in which there were important, positively portrayed characters from the dominant culture. Although they were developed very differently, both were strong, white, male characters. Although Frikke is a prominent character, Tromper is clearly a supporting character. Seven of nine students—four girls and three boys—who read *Waiting for the Rain* assumed the role of Frikke, and two of thirteen—both boys—who read *Finding My Voice* wrote as Tromper.

Although beyond the range of this book, it is interesting to speculate on why these two characters were the only dominant-culture characters chosen. *Waiting for the Rain* is written by a European American woman; *Finding My Voice* is written by a Korean American woman. *Waiting for the Rain* is written in the third person and appears to present two viewpoints—white South African and black South African—without bias. Frikke is the nephew of the owner of a large farm and is inheritor of the land. Tengo is black, with all the attendant implications of apartheid South Africa. He is a kaffir (disparaging term for black person) and son of the foreman—or boss-boy—and the house maid on the farm owned by Frikke's uncle. Yet, at the end, the status quo prevails—Frikke still cannot understand the struggle, whereas Tengo, supposedly in the name of nonviolence, lets his white friend live even though doing so is a betrayal of his family, his friends, and the greater cause of equality. *Finding My Voice* is written in the first person and clearly reflects the perspective of Ellen, a Korean American high school girl. Tromper is the white, golden-haired, varsity heartthrob who has his choice of girls and chooses Ellen over the dominant-culture cheerleader. *Waiting for the Rain*, set in South Africa, reflects struggles outside the United States, and thus, ostensibly, foreign to the readers in Ann's classes. Perhaps, however, readers imposed their perceptions of race relations within the United States on the apartheid situation in South Africa. *Finding My Voice* is set in a small Minnesota town and involves life in a high school similar in many ways to the one attended by Ann's students.

Readers' Perceptions of Characters

One of the most interesting findings of this study pertained to readers' perceptions of the nondominant characters in the books they read. As in the earlier discussion about worldview, the results of this question for the Book Club Organizer and the Dialogue Journal were remarkably similar, even though one assignment was a fairly traditional fill-in-the-blank school assignment and appeared to require an efferent stance, whereas the other involved creating a narrative from a character's perspective, presumably inviting an aesthetic stance.

Denying Difference

In both their Book Club Organizer and their Dialogue Journal, slightly more than 50% of students failed to recognize that being part of nondominant cultures had an impact on characters and their actions. Although it was clearly not the case in the novels they read, students assumed that characters of nondominant cultures had freedom to act in the same ways that dominant-culture characters or the readers would have. Readers didn't perceive the societal limitations imposed on people because of their cultural affiliation. They failed to recognize the disadvantages, constraints, and challenges involved in being part of nondominant cultures. Students assumed that characters from nondominant cultures were free to act without the constraints imposed by systems favoring the dominant culture. This assumption enabled Bob to describe Tengo in *Waiting for the Rain* as a "slave boy on Oom Koos's farm" who "deals with racial stress" while at the same time permitting Bob to assume that Tengo was free to do as he chose: "Tengo gets and reads his books.... Tengo decides to go to school.... Tengo goes to school." The same assumption enabled Beth to recognize Maria's illegal immigrant status in *Journey of the Sparrows* yet to assume, without recognizing the dire consequences, that Maria could simply quit her job if she chose: "They went across the border from Mexico...in a crate.... Maria's boss tried to touch her in bad places so she quit."

Assuming Superiority

In their Book Club Organizers and Dialogue Journals, less than 5% of students appeared paternalistic. Paternalism is a type of arrogance that permits people in power positions to act as defenders or saviors. These people often exhibit a condescending attitude, either implicitly or explicitly. Students who exhibited a paternalistic attitude defended other cultural groups (e.g., "not all blacks are in gangs"), explained behavior (e.g., "immigration is tough"), or provided an altruistic rationalization (e.g., "racism harms everyone"). Julie's explanation of illegal immigrant life hinted strongly of paternalism when she wrote in her Dialogue Journal, "It's so hard for me. I work all day and rarely travel really far away.... *Journey of the Sparrows* showed our life like it was, the joys and troubles. How we were struggling to survive in a country foreign to us."

Readers writing from this perspective often saw characters from the nondominant group as downtrodden or victimized. Sometimes readers' idealism enabled them to ignore difficulties experienced by nondominant groups or to consider those difficulties as isolated incidents. Sometimes readers displayed an altruistic attitude as Jason did in his Post-Unit Survey when he wrote,

> South Africans are very good in sports. Many are judges or political figures.... Some [people from Pakistan] are very highly educated people with good jobs and good lives.... Many [Chinese Americans] are great figure skaters or authors.... Many African Americans are very talented in sports.... Some [Latino Americans] are very wealthy and successful.... Some [Vietnamese Americans] are very accomplished people and lead wonderful lives.... Many [Korean Americans] are very kind people and very successful.

Responses like Jason's merely resulted in replacing one stereotype with another, albeit a more positive one. Often, such readers tended to insist that all people are the same, but they revealed their unconscious bias when they consistently used "us"—meaning white Americans—as the norm against which others were compared.

In their Book Club Organizers and Dialogue Journals, almost 15% of students appeared to consider the characters as "other," indicating an us-versus-them perspective: "They are in gangs"; "they are illegal immigrants"; "they are black." Rather than denying differences, these readers denied similarities. Students indicated that others might be gang members, immigrants, blacks, or merely "those people." Consider the responses of Carrie and Sally. After reading *Shabanu*, Carry noted, "We have god; they have Allah"; and after reading *Scorpions*, Sally wrote in her Book Club Organizer that the book promotes the stereotypes that "Blacks are poor. Blacks are trouble. Blacks are in gangs." Yet when explaining what she observed about the world in which the characters lived, Sally appeared to operate with that stereotype when she answered "that most blacks are poor," but in her Post-Unit Survey, she said she was happy that she got to read *Scorpions* because "I liked it a lot. I thought it was true to black life."

Recognizing the Struggles of Dealing With a Dual Identity

Only a third of the students recognized that nondominant characters had to deal with two different cultures simultaneously and that they lived with a dual identity that required them to be part of separate yet overlapping cultural situations. Although Danny, the Vietnamese American boy in *Shadow of the Dragon*, dates blond, blue-eyed Tiffany, he also must defend himself against Tiffany's brother, a skinhead who attacks Danny because of his ethnicity, and he must try to rescue two girls, recently arrived from Vietnam, who are being harassed by whites. Another example of a character with a dual identity is

Shabanu, a female in a male-dominated society. Because she is female, Shabanu is allowed to care for her family's camels only until she is old enough to marry. At that time, she must marry and assume her societal role, leaving her beloved camels to her male counterparts.

In the Book Club Organizer, Aaron actually acknowledged the concept of dual identity when he wrote that *Shadow of the Dragon* "might also say how hard it is for people to come into a new society or culture." Kathy, too, recognized the struggle in the same book when she first introduced herself as Danny in her Dialogue Journal:

> I am Vietnamese.... When I first entered the American schools, I hate to admit it now, but I pretended I was Chinese so that no one would ask me questions about the war. I wasn't even born until after the war.

Recognizing Norms, Values, and Cultural Markers

Although 80% of Ann's students consciously or unconsciously noted obvious aspects of nondominant cultures such as food preferences or skin color, 75% also indicated more sophisticated understandings of underlying cultural differences such as family relationships and responsibilities, age and gender roles, and religious beliefs and the impact of those beliefs on the everyday lives of people. However, that does not mean that students necessarily recognized them as aspects of the cultures or could translate these norms and values into an appropriate cultural worldview. For example, identifying culture-specific gender roles in a story didn't mean that students necessarily recognized them as characteristic of the culture or recognized how they affected the characters' lives. When Brad wrote, "Many practice religions different than ours; I think some of the religions are a little strange but that's probably because I'm only used to my religion," we can assume that he understands that cultural groups practice religions different from his, although he doesn't understand specifically how or what this means. Sometimes readers attributed inappropriate characteristics to cultural groups. For example, when Ricky stated, "Chinese Americans save money to buy things" without including supporting details or a concrete context, it was clear that his response was stereotypical.

However, 25% of readers did not appear to recognize cultural markers at all or, if they did, appeared to see them merely as idiosyncrasies of individual people or families and not as characteristic of particular cultures. When describing characters in *Shadow of the Dragon*, Nick mentioned that Danny skips a date to find his sister, the grandmother is old-fashioned and very religious,

Hong is old-fashioned with no use for American girls, and Kim wants to fit in with American girls. However, Nick gave no indication that he consciously recognized that any of these issues are related to culture; they "just are." And although Nick may have seen them as consistent with Danny's individual family situation, he didn't appear to recognize that these types of family interactions were characteristic of the Vietnamese cultural influence within the context of the story.

Sometimes, however, it is important to look beyond the obvious in students' responses. After reading *Scorpions*, Katie described Jamal as "very hyper and always getting in a lot of trouble" and Mama as "a very nice lady." Leigh described Jamal as "get[ting] in trouble a lot" and the "leader of the Scorpions" and depicted Mama as a woman who "works a lot has a lot of stress in her life." Although these responses seem quite similar on the surface, Leigh's response differed dramatically from Katie's because elsewhere in his writing Leigh revealed a recognition that the motivation for the characters' actions was their close family relationship. He wrote that the characters "care for people close to them" and that "their family and friends are very valued." When Leigh later said that this "compares to my culture because I care for my family and friends," it became clear that he saw these as characteristics of a culture, not merely idiosyncrasies of individual people or families as it appeared on a first reading.

Identifying With Characters Results in Transforming Them

In an exhaustive review of research on reader response, Purves and Beach (1972) found that readers often ascribe to characters values that aren't found in the story. They also misinterpret what they read if it conflicts with their own worldview. In fact, the more personally or intensely readers respond to the material they are reading, the more likely they are to interpret the author's intent inaccurately. So, just as authors write out of their own personal worldview, readers read out of theirs. Zimet (1976) notes that readers "process the text in order to meet [their] own personal needs. In doing so, [they] may extend or merely confirm [their] already existing repertoire of ideas, attitudes and behaviours" (pp. 16–17).

Reading students' papers from Ann's classes made it clear to me how difficult it is to see from another's viewpoint. Because of the unearned privilege of being white, whites can't imagine not being white, which makes it virtually impossible to identify with the characters in a book who are from nondominant cultures. Instead, when I read, I transform the characters into "me." When

I "identify" with them, I fool myself into thinking that I become them, but, in reality, I make them into me. But being me is dramatically different from being them.

People with power can't imagine what it's like to be without power. In *Black Like Me*, Griffin (1961) provides the best description I know of what it might be like. An educated man, a novelist, a newspaper reporter, and white, Griffin "became" black. He shaved his head, took medication to change the color of his skin, and moved to New Orleans, Louisiana. He survived in New Orleans and other southern U.S. towns for six weeks. Although he was a "specialist in race relations" (p. 8), he found himself in a world he previously had thought he could imagine, but which he found to be totally different from anything he could conceive of—a world in which he experienced hate, fear, and hopelessness beyond anything he had imagined. In the book's preface Griffin writes, "I could have been a Jew in Germany, a Mexican in a number of states, or a member of any 'inferior' group. Only the details would have differed. The story would be the same" (p. 5). In the end of the book, Griffin returns to his white world transformed by his experience. Some readers will be changed by the books they read; however, just as Griffin is white and could return to that world, white readers always can step out of the lives of the nondominant characters and return to the world of the dominant culture. White readers really cannot imagine what it means to be nonwhite—all day—every day of their lives. Because of that, they cannot understand what it means to be part of nondominant cultures.

Learning That Did Not Transfer

On the first two assignments, students wrote about specific characters in the books they read, but on the Post-Unit Survey, they wrote about people—not characters—from various cultures. On the Post-Unit Surveys, readers' responses changed dramatically. Although writing from the Book Club Organizers and Dialogue Journals revealed only a small percentage of students were paternalistic toward characters from nondominant cultures, the Post-Unit Surveys revealed that 32% of students were paternalistic toward actual people of those cultures. On further comparison of students' writing, I realized that in their Book Club Organizers and Dialogue Journals, 13% to 17% of students, respectively, considered characters of nondominant cultures to be "other," but in the Post-Unit Surveys, 50% of students appeared to see people of nondominant cultures as "other." Writing in students' Book Club Organizers and Dialogue Journals showed that about 53% of students assumed that characters of nondominant cultures have the same freedom to act as they themselves have, which, in effect, ignored the constraints society places on people of nondominant cultures. On the Post-Unit Survey, however, only 6% of students accorded people from nondominant cultures the same freedom to act as they themselves have, which in effect, demonstrated a lack of awareness of the constraints society places on people of nondominant cultures. Finally, rather than 29% and 28% of students who recognized in their Book Club Organizers and Dialogue Journals, respectively, that people from nondominant cultures have to deal simultaneously with two different cultures, only 6% of students recognized that reality in their Post-Unit Surveys. The exact percentages are included here because they indicate a dramatic discrepancy. Although the students came to know literary characters, they continued to stereotype actual people from nondominant cultures.

Graham (1985), too, found strong resistance to change. She studied five white high school sophomores from blue-collar families. Faced with an influx of Vietnamese students into their school, these students "were not adapting to the cultural change in their community and school" (p. 1). When the students had strong biases that conflicted with ideas they read in texts, they either rejected the ideas or reshaped them. According to Graham, they did so even when that reshaping "resulted in inconsistencies or illogical conclusions" (p. 165). She suggests that teachers use "carefully guided discussions of texts, not to direct students toward a single approved reading, but to invite them to examine their otherwise unchallenged assumptions" (p. 165).

Reflective of Heath's (1983) findings in her classic study of the influence of students' home communities on their educational achievement, Graham comments in the introduction,

> One of adolescents' predicaments today is the attitudinal rigidity that traps them in their perceptions of the world. While being exposed to different cultures, they often continue to hold tightly to the attitudes and behaviors instilled by their own cultural group. Rather than adapting to their changing world and environment to realize "a new perception of things," they seem to react on presuppositions inherited from their parents and their culture, presuppositions that may be based on intolerance, resistance to change, and hostility. (p. 1)

Beach and Freedman (1992) also suggest that readers' responses may be shaped more by the particular cultural identities transmitted by their local communities than by peers, as is typically assumed:

Based on 10 years of research with adolescents in 10 different American communities, Francis Ianni (1989) questions the force of a homogeneous, national youth culture. He found a wide diversity in adolescents' peer groups attitudes and values that are more likely to mirror the diversity of background parent and community attitudes and values, undermining the force of a national "youth culture." Adolescents from poorer families and communities were quite different from those in affluent communities. The peer group "youth cultures" were often linked to various adult institutions that shaped the attitudes of those youth cultures. For example, the ways in which relationships were structured in peer groups reflected the attitudes of the community culture. (p. 165)

Beach and Freedman argue that the attitudes of adolescents may be consistent with or in conflict with these values but cannot be independent of them. Instead, they suggest that responses may be shaped by the particular cultural practices adolescents acquire. When Beach and Freeman asked 115 eighth and eleventh graders from two middle-class suburban communities to respond to advertisements and stories involving various levels of gender stereotyping, they discovered that students were much more likely to respond emotionally to characters in stories than to models in magazine advertisements. The researchers surmised that this may have been because the stories permitted students to experience and, thus, empathize with the perspectives of the characters. However, the students were more likely to like and positively rate the models in the advertisements, whom they admired from a distance and whom they perceived to have power, success, or status, but whose perspectives they didn't experience. Similar to these students, Ann's readers responded emotionally to the stories they read and empathized with the characters, but they also remained locked in rigidly stratified perceptions of the real world.

Teachers need to recognize that readers seldom truly identify with a character. The research shows that when readers identify with characters, they assume not that they are the characters but that the characters are like them. In essence, they appear to re-create the characters in their own images. Like Griffin (1961), who thought he could imagine what it meant to be a black man, dominant-culture readers think that they understand the lives of nondominant characters. However, readers don't enter the world of characters in the same way as Griffin did. Instead, readers create the story world in the way the world appears to them—not the way it really is. And, at the end of the story, readers leave the worlds of nondominant groups and return to that of the dominant group. Although they may be transformed by their experience, as Griffin was, we cannot assume that readers from the dominant culture learn what it's like to be someone else just by participating in personal experiences with a story.

Ann's students were much more likely to recognize cultural norms, values, or markers when completing assignments related to their books, and they were less likely to recognize cultural norms, values, or markers when they were asked about peoples of cultures different from their own. For example, after reading *Finding My Voice*, Jolyn explained the story world by providing concrete examples from the Korean American main character's life experiences. In her Book Club Organizer, she wrote, "They strongly believe in doing well, getting good grades, going to the best school. I also learned that they had a hard life. They are constantly fighting our society because of their race." However, in her Post-Unit Survey she reverted back to common stereotypes when explaining the positive things she knew or believed about Korean Americans. After stating she knew that South Africans, Chinese Americans, and Vietnamese (although she was asked about Vietnamese Americans) were peaceful and that South Africans and Latino Americans were good at making crafts, she wrote that Korean Americans were "again, peaceful people. Great at crafts and lettering."

Although the tendency to know characters concretely but know cultural groups stereotypically was a consistent finding in Ann's students' work, the students did recognize cultural norms, values, or cultural markers in their Book Club Organizers more often than they did in their Dialogue Journals when they assumed the roles of characters. Perhaps working together with other readers to complete their Book Club Organizers provided students with information they didn't have when they wrote individually in their Dialogue Journals. If so, it would indicate that the book clubs had a positive effect on student learning. Not surprising, readers who recognized unique cultural values and norms in their Book Club Organizers usually recognized them in their Dialogue Journals and Post-Unit Surveys. Those who recognized specific cultural markers in their Book Club Organizers usually recognized them in the other two assignments, too (the hypothesis test of binomial proportion indicated a statistical significance of $p < .01$ and $p < .06$, respectively). It is disturbing, though, that students' understanding of cultures in assignments related to literature didn't appear to carry over to the assignment that asked what they knew about actual people of a cultural group. In Table 2, note the high percentage of students who gave evidence of learning about aspects of culture in literature, but the low percentage of students who indicated the same learning when asked about people.

Table 2.   Evidence of Cultural Understanding in Three Assignments

Book Club Organizer (literature)	Dialogue Journal (literature)	Post-Unit Survey (people)	Reader Response
75.4%	57.3%	42.7%	Readers who gave evidence of conscious recognition of the norms and values of a culture different from their own
73.9%	65.3%	44.1%	Readers who recognized markers specific to a particular culture

Readers Perceived Stories as Anomalies

Throughout this section, I have explained that readers in Ann's classes recognized aspects of culture in the books they were reading, but little if any of their learning appeared to transfer to their Post-Unit Survey. In chapter 2, I noted that the general assumption of educators has been that reading multicultural literature will cause dominant-culture readers to become more knowledgeable about people from other cultures and more accepting of diversity. However, in this study it appeared that Ann's students were employing what Allport (1954/1958) refers to as "re-fencing":

> [There is a] common mental device that permits people to hold to prejudgments even in the fact of much contradictory evidence. It is the device of admitting exceptions. "There are nice Negoes, but..." or "Some of my best friends are Jews but...." This is a disarming device. By excluding a few favored cases, the negative rubric is kept intact for all other cases. In short, contrary evidence is not admitted and allowed to modify the generalization; rather it is perfunctorily acknowledged but excluded. (p. 23)

Ann's students became involved with the stories and developed a special fondness for the characters. But they saw the characters and their situations as anomalies, or unique incidences not characteristic of the world in general. By re-fencing, they were able to like the characters and sympathize with their situations without having to modify their existing schema for thinking about people of nondominant cultures. Ann's students were able to see each story as an isolated incident, and, because it was an isolated incident, they saw no reason to rethink their existing perceptions or stereotypes of people from other cultures.

If this is indeed what happened, it is clear that, as a teacher, Ann acted on the principles of best practice, but the principles themselves were flawed. The assumptions about what would happen by having dominant-culture readers read multicultural literature were different from what actually happened. Ann did have her students read multicultural literature, but doing so did not achieve her goal of having them understand the impact of being nonwhite in the United States. They recognized, to some extent, the impact in the story, but by seeing the story as an anomaly, they were able to ignore the impact in the real world.

Barbara Tobin (1989) discovered a similar pattern when she studied the responses of 14 male and 14 female, upper–middle-class, urban, white, Australian seventh graders (ages 11 years, 8 months, to 12 years, 7 months) of mixed academic abilities. Just as Ann's readers failed to make links between the story world and the real world, Tobin notes of the readers in her study, "[I]t seemed as if, without specifically directed classroom discussion, that the students were not making the links from current affairs to literature, from the outside world to school experiences" (p. 170). In spite of widespread media coverage of issues closely related to the theme of the book they were reading, none of Tobin's students connected the news reports with their reading. Furthermore, when the "readers were left to read and respond to these books without the benefit of peer group discussion, and/or teacher guidance, there was no chance for the readers to appreciate the cultural implications and understandings intended by the author" (p. 312). Even though Tobin's students had significant background knowledge and preparation for their reading, she felt that "their own cultural attitudes and expectations, based on their own past experiences with life and literature...originating in an upper–middle-class urban area dominated by White cultural values and experiences" (pp. 312–316), did not permit them to recognize the full meaning and significance of the text.

Tobin concludes that teachers need to provide "gentle guidance by the provision of thought provoking points of reflection, and opportunities to share and reshape interpretations" (p. 320) if the goal is to help students understand and appreciate the cultural richness of the text. She suggests that teachers first provide an opportunity for students' private responses; then have students share reactions and interpretations within a small, supportive peer group—sometimes focused by teacher guidance; and finally have students share in "the collective reading experience of the classroom community of readers" (p. 320). Tobin had students use free response writing in a journal, which appears similar in many ways to the thinkbook used by Ann's students throughout the year. She also provided topics for students to think and write about if they couldn't think of anything on their own. Tobin responded to the students' writing, occasionally posing questions to the readers. She found that most students enjoyed this interaction and found it helpful. As a researcher, she was able to determine students' strengths and limitations in comprehending and responding to text. Based on the students' failure to use their existing knowledge, Tobin suggests that teachers need to help students integrate their learning across curricular areas by specifically connecting new experiences, such as reading a new novel, with prior experiences, such as school-based learning and media exposure. Tobin concluded that, because the school learning of many white students is superficial and because they lack real life experience, their ability to apply school learning beyond the curriculum is limited. She encourages teachers to arrange cultural experiences reflecting alternative perspectives that will break down racial stereotypes and enable readers to better recognize the "invisible" (p. 326) culture when they meet it in literature. In Tobin's study, the active involvement of the teacher again emerges as an important component of teaching multicultural literature.

Readers' Understanding of Themselves Did Not Increase

Ann's second goal for students was to increase their understanding of themselves and their own cultural norms or values, but as I repeatedly read the students' papers, I could not find evidence that this occurred. Instead, I found that students thought about their own culture's norms and values as a given. In fact, they seldom explicitly recognized that they belonged to a particular culture or had norms and values. When Applebee (1978) studied children's understanding of stories, he discovered that

> it is not until adolescence...that spectator-role language begins to be recognized as offering simply a possible view of the world, one among many interpretations...the early adolescent often rejects works which are not realistic presentations of the world as he or she sees it. Only gradually...are the conventions of fantasy and the possibilities inherent in alternative views of the world accepted freely and openly. (p. 133)

Although Applebee is referring to fantasy literature, multicultural literature also requires the reader to create worlds that are not realistic presentations of the world as he or she sees it. The readers in Ann's classes, although in eighth grade, were exhibiting the responses characteristic of younger children and early adolescents. Rather than recognizing their own worldview as one alternative among many, students didn't seem to realize that others' worldviews could be significantly different from their own. If this is the case, it would account, in part, for Ann's feeling that her students hadn't learned about other cultures. Although they frequently talked about the way characters and people from other cultures thought, they seldom appeared to recognize that they were implicitly comparing the norms and values of other cultures to their own. When students reflected on their own values and norms at all, it was usually in response to a direct question from Ann. For example, responding to a question in the Book Club Organizer about how the character's world in *Shabanu* compared or contrasted with her own world, Sandra commented, "We don't get married until about 20. I don't know why, but parents think we are too young and don't know anything."

Even when asked to compare a character's world and values to their own in the Book Club Organizers, only 35% of students reflected any evidence of increased understanding of their own world. On assignments that did not direct them explicitly to compare the character's world to their own, fewer showed an increase in understanding of their own world: Less than 10% showed any increase in the Dialogue Journals, and only 3% did so on the Post-Unit Surveys. Although this means Ann's goal of having students recognize their own cultural norms and values was not achieved by the time the unit was over, Ann may have initiated a process of change. For example, Galda (1992), in a case study of eight readers, found that as readers mature and learn more about literature, they became better able to view texts as possible realities and to understand them in terms of the story world rather than what they know about the real world. If this is true of readers in general, it is likely that Ann helped her students move closer to understanding that their individual worldviews are not the norm for everyone.

However, Ann's students had not achieved this goal by the end of the unit. Instead, 50% of readers assumed that characters with ethnic identities other than white had the same freedom to act as they themselves did; thus, they were unable to enter the characters' world. Instead, they assumed that the characters lived lives like people from their own culture: They re-created characters in their own images. They failed to recognize the privileges they enjoyed because they were white. In effect, they negated Ann's very purpose for having them read multicultural literature in the first place. Only 60% appeared to be reading in what Jordan and Purves (1993) call "the spirit of the culture" (p. 2). Instead, similar to early adolescents in Applebee's (1978) study, Ann's students appeared to accept their worldviews as *the* view. In fact, Ann's students actually appeared to interact with the literature just as partners do in face-to-face conversation. They "[assumed] a common representation or worldview from the start...[and] in the end, they...fitted the story into their worldview, assimilated it.... In a very real sense, they...[had] *given it* the meaning which it will have for them" (1978, p. 7).

Readers Did Not Challenge Texts

When planning the unit, Ann realized that she would need to encourage and support readers in questioning both the content of the book they read and the authors' presentation of that content. Although she tried to do this, her students' papers gave little evidence that they went beyond aesthetic responses to read against the text. Occasionally, before asking them to write in their Dialogue Journals, Ann would invite readers to think about an author's ethnic background or an author's experiences related to the story. Then on the day students finished their Dialogue Journals, she also asked them to explain if they thought their books were authentic representations of cultures reflected in them. In spite of such encouragement, only 26 of 73 students (35%) questioned the content in the books or the authors' presentation when writing in their Dialogue Journals. In their Book Club Organizers, the more traditional school assignment in which we would expect readers to assume efferent stances toward reading and, thus, to think about the validity of the material and to compare the content with other information, only 15 of 69 students (22%) questioned or challenged the content or authors of their novels. Much more disturbing than these numbers, however, is that only 5 of 60 (p < .00001) students who completed both their Book Club Organizers and their Dialogue Journals challenged or questioned any aspect of the reflection of the non-dominant culture in the novels read.

The few readers who did reflect on the authenticity of their novels did so in interesting ways and for different reasons. When explaining the author's point of view in *Shadow of the Dragon* and suggesting reasons why the author chose that point of view, Bruce suggested that she "might of chose that because she really didn't know their background." Dee was much more straightforward in her challenge of the text. When asked what stereotypes are promoted in *Journey of the Sparrows*, Dee wrote, "Mexicans are poor. They are drunk rappers [rapists]. That they are bad." Although she buys into a stereotype by assuming that the novel is about Mexican rather than Guatemalan characters, Dee still recognized that these are stereotypes and wrote that the book is not an authentic representation of the culture because "lots is not true. Not all the culture are like that." Dee also commented, "This book was pretty accurate in showing what people go through if they are illegal aliens but it made you have a lot of sympathy for them.... Their culture is portrayed poor and uneducated which isn't true." Kathy asked thoughtful questions in her Dialogue Journal as she wrote about *Shadow of the Dragon*:

> I think the culture authenticity is somewhat true and untrue. When it comes to the story about a dragon and princess and about their ancestors, it's hard to believe, but I bet that is what the Vietnamese believe. I don't know for sure. There are many superstitions, that I can only question. Who knows if they're true? I think the book does show there is racism when it comes to interacial dating. It does give out a stereotype that Vietnamese are communist, but it says that Danny and his family aren't. What am I supposed to believe? The book shows how Kim is a rebel and dresses sleezy, but I'm sure not everyone who [is Vietnamese] has a sister [who] is like that.... The book also shows how the grandmother is very pushy and opinionated and doesn't like American cultures. She must be old fashioned and stuck with her own ways, but not everyone is like that.... I think lots of the culture authenticity is questionable.

Finding *Shabanu* to be a generally favorable cultural representation, Lydie still noted that

> the author was viewing the culture as an outsider and I think they did a good job in making the book as authentic as they could. They used the correct words and name of objects...in a way the characters were presented somewhat weirdly. The author stressed a lot on the clothing they wore and it really wasn't very important in the story. It seemed like the author thought their clothing was kind of weird.

Ralph wasn't very sure about the authenticity of *Waiting for the Rain* because he wrote, "I don't know [if the novel is an authentic representation of the culture]. It focuses around only one family. [These] characters...are the only ones thruought the book." Donald, on the other hand, thought that the culture in *Shadow of the Dragon* "[was] well represented but a bit agzagerated."

Increases in Cultural Understanding

To determine whether students had increased their understanding of cultural groups other than their own, raters compared students' responses on the Pre- and Post-Unit Surveys. The following responses were considered evidence that a reader had increased in cultural understanding during the unit. Demonstrating such a response about any one cultural group was considered sufficient to indicate an increase in cultural understanding.

- A student became more realistic and relied less on generalized or stereotypical statements.

Example: Ben learned from group presentations that South Africans "work hard for a living and [have] good family beleives." On the Pre-Unit Survey, he had answered that South Africans are "good hunters."

- A student moved from long, stereotypical or naive statements to realizing "I don't know" or "I don't know much about [people belonging to a specific group]."

Example: Ted first wrote, "I think [Native Americans] are good at making things. It just seems like they can make nice stuff like bracelets and blankets," but then acknowledged that "I don't know anything about them."

- A student provided more specific responses about a particular culture. (Even if the specific response appeared to be negative, it was considered more realistic than a naive platitude.)

Example: Before reading her novel, Sissy wrote, "I can't specifically say that I know a lot about people from South Africa—I know they are black. I think this is common knowledge. I guess I'm assuming that since they're from Africa, they must be black." At the end of the unit, she said, "I know that they are patient and enjoy learning. I learned this from reading the book *Waiting for the Rain*."

- A student's response realistically reflected information in one of the books read, even if the response appeared to be negative.

Example: A response such as "Some Vietnamese hate Americans" might be very realistic for a student who had read *Shadow of the Dragon* because, in that book, the grandmother clearly expresses her disapproval of much that is American. (On the other hand, "Vietnamese hate Americans because of the war" would be classified as negative and stereotypical if given by a student who had read *Scorpions* and whose responses about other groups reflected similar stereotyping.)

Although statements such as "Not all blacks are in gangs," "Racism harms everyone," or "Immigration is tough" sound good, they usually were considered paternalistic, stereotypical, or both, because in context of the students' other writings, such statements were used as platitudes and seldom reflected understanding. Responses on the Post-Unit Surveys indicated that half of Ann's students had increased their understanding of at least one nondominant culture or were more positive, although they still may have been stereotypical, toward cultural groups other than their own. The other students demonstrated little, if any, change in their responses from the Pre- to Post-Unit Survey. Although almost 40% of Ann's students were still either paternalistic or negatively stereotypical in their responses on the Post-Unit Survey, it was encouraging that none of the students were more negative in their stereotyping than they had been on the Pre-Unit Surveys.

Cultural Understanding and Its Relation to Response

Chapter 1 highlighted the apparent conflict between aesthetic reading and the role of multicultural literature. One of the most important questions facing teachers today is the same conflict Ann faced in this unit. We want children to like to read, to enjoy reading, and to enter the world of a book and lose themselves in it. We also want children to learn about people different from themselves, and we hope that literature will help them do this. But does it? What is the relationship between aesthetic response and cultural understanding? Researchers have explored many aspects of this question. For example, when Cox and Many (1992) studied fourth through eighth graders, they found that "when readers focused on the lived-through experience of most stories, their reported responses were consistently richer in understanding" (p. 118). This led them to conclude that "understanding reader stance…[is] more than picking your own library book. It requires centering the literature teaching experience in the literary responses of readers" (p. 124).

Although it is difficult to determine just how much of Ann's teaching was centered on students' responses, it is clear that Ann incorporated their responses much more in this unit than she had in previous units and classes. Previously, she accepted and validated students' responses but insisted that the students focus on the literature rather than themselves. Ann functioned as the interpretive authority in the classroom. Her primary goal for the multicultural literature unit, however, was that students enjoy reading and understanding their multicultural novels. Although she intended to move them beyond their personal responses, she gave the students significant responsibility for interpretation of the literature. Working together in literature discussion groups, students read their novels and used their Book Club Organizers to summarize the literary and cultural aspects of their books. In the Dialogue Journals, each student assumed the identity of a character in the book and wrote back and forth to a classmate who had read a different novel. And, in book clubs, students developed a class presentation about their book.

By combining scores from selected questions on the Evaluation Instrument, I created two composite scores for each student: one to reflect the student's aesthetic response and one to reflect the student's cultural understanding at the end of the unit. I compared the combined scores to determine whether students with high scores for aesthetic response also had high scores for cultural understanding. In statistical terms, I wanted to know if a correlation existed between aesthetic response and cultural understanding. The raters' evaluations of student papers in response to the following criteria were used to create a composite score for aesthetic response. (The numbers following each statement indicate the questions on the Evaluation Instrument [see Appendix E] that were used as the basis for determining the student's score on that particular item. Numbers 6–19 pertain to the Book Club Organizer, numbers 20–32 pertain to the Dialogue Journal, and numbers 33–44 pertain to the Post-Unit Survey.)

- The reader felt positively about reading the novel [6].
- The reader would choose to read another novel with characters who have different backgrounds and histories from his or her own [7].
- The reader clearly was operating in the story world when writing from the perspective of a character [20].
- The reader enjoyed the book (only scores for the Post-Unit Survey [36] could be used because there was no variation in readers' responses on the Book Club Organizers [8] or the Dialogue Journals [23], i.e., all students enjoyed the books).

The raters' evaluations of student papers in response to the following criteria were used to create a composite score for cultural understanding:

- The reader appeared to recognize that the actions and reactions of the primary character(s) from the nondominant cultures emanated from a worldview different from that of the dominant culture [9, 24, 37].
- The reader recognized that the nondominant-culture character needed to operate, simultaneously, with two different sets of cultural expectations [10, 25, 38].
- The reader did not generalize from the nondominant characters in the book to all members of the characters' cultural group, unless asked to do so in the assignment [11, 26].

- The reader's conscious or unconscious learning about the non-dominant culture reflected in the book tended toward a realistic understanding rather than a stereotypical one [13, 28].
- The reader consciously recognized the norms and values of a culture different from his or her own [14, 29, 41].
- The reader recognized unique characteristics such as family patterns and responsibilities, age and gender expectations, or the role of religion, as aspects of particular cultures [17, 32, 44].
- The reader understood, implicitly or explicitly, the impact ethnicity had on the lives of the characters from the nondominant cultures [21].
- The reader, when writing from the perspective of a character from a nondominant culture, revealed the character's struggles, motivations, and actions that occurred because of the character's culture [22].
- The reader's responses on the Post-Unit Survey appear to reflect the nondominant culture accurately [34].
- The reader's responses on the Post-Unit Survey are different from responses on the Pre-Unit Survey, appearing to reflect the nondominant culture more accurately [35].
- The reader acknowledges variation within the nondominant cultural group [39].
- The reader's conscious or unconscious learning about the nondominant culture appears to have become more realistic on the Post-Unit Survey than it was on the Pre-Unit Survey [40].

Using a statistical test called the Pearson Product Moment Correlation, I calculated what is known as the Pearson Correlation Coefficient. The coefficient, or number, indicates the degree of relationship between the way a student responds aesthetically to a book he or she has read and how much the student understands about the culture reflected in that book. I calculated the relationship for each assignment separately. I also combined each student's scores for the three assignments (this is his or her total score for understanding) and compared that with his or her aesthetic score (see Table 3).

I concluded that the readers who had strong aesthetic responses to their books also learned the most about the cultures. All the correlations are statistically significant, which simply means that the relationship in each could not have happened by chance. The finding is particularly encouraging because it confirms, again, Rosenblatt's argument that reader response is primary, and

Table 3. Relationship Between Aesthetic Response and Cultural Understanding

Assignments	Relationship Between Students' Aesthetic Response and Their Understanding of the Culture, Represented as a Correlation Coefficient (r)	Level of Significance
Book Club Organizer	.34	.0052
Dialogue Journal	.25	.0322
Post-Unit Survey	.33	.0065
Total Score for Understanding	.59	< .0001

this is where teachers must begin. The finding also indicates that despite readers' tendency to "read what they are," that is, to re-create characters in their own images, teachers can influence the learning outcome of students who read multicultural literature in the classroom.

Perhaps the most important relationship I found, however, was in Ann's evaluation of her students' learning. I found a stronger relationship between the students' total scores for understanding and the grades Ann assigned her students at year's end than between the students' total scores for understanding and their scores on the California Test of Basic Skills (CTBS) for reading, language, and math ($p < .012$). Ann knew her students and knew what they had learned. Although this will not surprise most teachers, it is another indication that no standardized test can take the place of a teacher's knowledge about his or her students.

What the Students Learned

At the beginning of the chapter, I asked whether Ann had achieved the culture-related objectives she had designed for the unit, and I said the answer was both yes and no. My findings show that the students made little connection between literary characters and people in real life. Although students could write from characters' viewpoints, reflecting the impact of ethnicity, they still assumed that nondominant-culture characters had the same freedom to act that dominant-culture characters or readers would have. Students did not perceive the societal limitations dominant-culture society imposes on people because of their ethnicity, and therefore, students failed to recognize the disadvantages, constraints, and challenges involved in being part of nondominant cultures. As students came to know characters as people, they did not identify with the characters. Instead, they assumed that the character was like them. In order to confirm their existing ideas, attitudes, and behaviors, students interpreted the texts in ways that allowed them to re-create the characters in their own images.

The tendency to know characters concretely but cultural groups stereotypically was another finding in the students' work. By treating stories as anomalies, students could respond emotionally to the stories and sympathize with the characters while maintaining rigidly stratified perceptions of the real world. They could come to know characters but continue to stereotype people. And for these readers, reading a multicultural novel didn't cause them to learn much about themselves, their norms, or their values, because they thought about their own culture's norms and values as givens.

Ann achieved her goal of having students recognize that characters from nondominant cultures were individuals who thought, spoke, acted, and reacted using the norms and values of their own cultures, but the students didn't transfer this recognition to real-life people. She wanted her students to see people from nondominant cultures as individuals with a full range of human experiences, who were affected by being nonwhite in the United States, but not merely victims. Her students did come to see characters of nondominant cultures as fully rounded individuals with a range of experiences, but they were not able to acknowledge the serious consequences of being nonwhite in the United States. Most students assumed that their perceptions of the world were the norm, and for the most part they accepted the author's portrayal of culture without question. In other words, they learned little about themselves and their assumptions.

Yes, Ann achieved her primary goal of having her students enjoy reading and understanding multicultural novels. And, yes, in doing so, she encouraged her students to learn about cultures other than their own. But, no, Ann's students didn't achieve all that she had hoped. Through it all, Ann's knowledge of her students and how much they were learning never faltered. Chapter 4 will focus on particular aspects of Ann's unit and make some suggestions for the next multicultural unit.

Concluding the Story: Looking Back and Looking Ahead

It takes great faith in learning and in the learning process not to become discouraged. There is often little concrete evidence of learning, and it is possible that the most learning takes place when the end products created are disappointing. (Ann)

As Ann reflected on the unit, she thought about what she would do differently next time. When she began the unit, Ann recognized that her students were far from achieving what she considered the most basic goals—of thinking critically and creatively and of understanding multiple points of view. Because of students' limited experience with texts that explored the issues surrounding culture and cultural dominance in today's world, they were unable to achieve this goal during the unit. For Ann, her students' inability to deal effectively with cultural differences was the most distressing aspect of the unit. She recognized that because students enjoyed the novels and saw what they were doing as valuable, few complained about the amount of work assigned—even the kind of work they generally disliked. But Ann also was convinced that the students' enjoyment of the novels did not automatically result in an accurate understanding of the cultures reflected in the books or in insight into their own lives as members of the dominant culture.

Challenges in Reading Multicultural Literature

Within the book clubs in the unit, students had more autonomy than usual. Yet implementing the book clubs simultaneously imposed time constraints on Ann that prohibited her from interacting with each group as much as she felt necessary. Remember that in her classroom, Ann had always been the interpretive authority, but during this unit, students worked together in small groups to develop comprehension and understanding of what they had read. Because she had seven different groups operating simultaneously during each class period, Ann was limited in the amount of time she spent with each group and also in the amount of input she had to book discussions. It is quite clear from students' work and Ann's journal that the only voice in the classroom community to contest, complement, or monitor the predominant view of the "other" was the teacher's. That voice was dramatically tempered because the book clubs used for the unit effectively prevented Ann from participating as an active member.

Many studies support the need for the teacher's voice. Zimet (1976) talks about many earlier studies in her book, *Print and Prejudice*. For example, Maccoby (in Zimet), found that the effects of media exposure on children's values, beliefs, and actions can be minimized by "counter-teaching, that is, by having available a broad variety of reading materials, expressing other viewpoints, by discussing the implications of the values presented, and by making explicit the range of other possible value positions" (p. 17). Fisher (in Zimet) demonstrates that there is a greater change in positive attitudes toward minorities when children (fifth graders) read stories and then participate in a teacher-led group discussion than when they simply read the stories. In discussing textbooks and other printed materials containing biases, Davies (in Zimet) suggests that students should have the opportunity to read materials expressing a variety of viewpoints and to discuss those materials "with skilled leadership from the teacher. In addition, teachers need to help their students acquire the reading analysis and comprehension skills that will enable them to differentiate fact from opinion, and to identify the author's bias" (p. 67).

The way the teacher approaches the material is important, however. Discussing a project designed to improve race relations throughout the secondary schools in England, Zimet (1976) explains that the Humanities Curriculum Project of the Schools Council used 200 written documents in a variety of formats reflecting a variety of viewpoints toward ethnic and racial groups. Citing Bagley's (1972) analysis of the material's effectiveness in changing students' attitudes, Zimet writes,

> In their handling of the race pack, teachers adopted a position of overt neutrality, not taking a dogmatic line in favour of tolerance or intolerance. Previous research on attitude change has in fact shown that dogmatism by a teacher in favour of a particular set of values is likely to be counterproductive. (p. 69)

According to Bagley (in Zimet), the results showed "that the teaching of race relations using the race pack was followed by moderate but unmistakable moves in the direction of the expressions of tolerant attitudes" (p. 69). Zimet concludes that studies of the use of books and materials designed to encourage a more pluralistic society have reported positive attitudes toward minority groups and that "classroom discussion of the ideas and issues raised by the content appear to play a crucial role in facilitating and fostering attitude change" (p. 70).

Kathy Short, a professor of Language, Reading and Culture at the University of Arizona (USA), received the International Reading Association's Arbuthnot Award for the year 2000 as the outstanding university teacher of children's and young adult literature. Advocating the use of literature circles (book clubs), she argues that reading curricula often leave out "engagements which focus on thoughtful analysis and talking in response to literature" (Mathis, 2001, p. 59). Short says, "Sometimes we forget the absolute importance of planning engagements that bring readers and books together in powerful ways" (p. 62). Ann planned these types of engagements in her class. But, as Short also notes, "It's not enough to just bring readers and books together in any way.... We must provide space for student response in a way that really honors that response but also challenges readers to think even more critically" (p. 62) through engaging them in dialogue, pushing their responses, and encouraging them to consider other perspectives.

Ann clearly recognized this need. Although she wanted students to think for themselves, she repeatedly attempted to challenge their thinking, especially when that thinking reflected easy, dominant-culture answers. For example, during the unit Ann introduced a poem, "When I Was Growing Up" (Wong, 1994), in which the poet reflects on the pain of growing up nonwhite in the United States. Discussing the poem pushed Ann's students to deal with questions of culture, cultural dominance, stereotypes, power differentials between cultural groups, and cultural privilege. After the unit, Ann recognized that the poem and the subsequent discussion were important but not sufficient. Incorporating additional resources and encouraging students to seek accurate information related to diverse cultures, particularly at the outset, would have prepared students to read their novels not just as stories but as more than stories. Cai (1998) points out the danger of failing to address the very issues that concerned Ann when she started the unit:

> If the response and discussion stops at seeking out the experiences that the
> reader has in common with the characters and does not examine closely the

social inequality and injustice caused by racism…it misses the point of reading about the Other. To see the commonalities among cultures is important, but to study the differences is equally important or even more important. Through discussion of differences…White students may become aware of their privilege and power…and also their bias…. How these students formed a negative image of [the Other] should be given serious attention (Bishop, 1994). If the issue is not addressed in their discussion of the book, the reading of the book is largely counterproductive even if they can relate to the story, because instead of removing the negative stereotype, the literary encounter perpetuates it. For all readers, reading various cultural messages in a book about people of color should not end at a narcissistic self-reflection but should eventually lead to changing their perspective on the Other. (p. 322)

In Ann's classes, only a few students became more aware of their privilege and power. Most failed to recognize that they had a negative image of "the Other." Although they liked their novels and, perhaps, related to the characters in the stories, their reading didn't change the stereotypes they held about other people. If anything, it appears that the readers declared the characters and stories to be anomalies, which permitted them to like their books and still keep intact their original view of people in cultures different from their own.

Rogers (1991) studied the relationship between how teachers teach literature and what students learn. To do this, she compared the literary experiences of eight ninth-grade students in two different "instructional subcommunities within their existing English classes" (p. 391). One group was led by the regular classroom teacher, who, like Ann, clearly possessed the social and interpretive authority and used few sources of information other than the text. The other group was led by Rogers, herself, and students were expected to share their responses and interpretations and to provide particulars from the literature and related material to support those interpretations. After hearing responses from their peers, students also were encouraged to reflect on their own responses. She concluded that "a reader's critical stance is highly individual…. [Readers are] influenced by a complex combination of their own beliefs about how literature should be interpreted, their literary experiences, and their abilities…" (p. 417). However, Rogers argues that more research is needed to understand the influence of interpretive communities on students' interpretive processes because she found strong evidence that students' preferences for ways of interpreting literature were affected by the way teachers taught. After students had participated in sessions in which they were expected to assume larger roles in interpreting the literature and expected to incorporate references to multiple "texts"—including comparisons to characters in other texts and to personal responses—students tended to prefer this style of interpretation over interpretation that focused on textual elements of a story during which the teacher was the social and interpretive authority.

The book clubs, or interpretive communities, in Ann's classroom appear to have exerted a powerful influence on the outcomes of the unit, too. However, in Rogers's study, the teacher in the experimental group was an influential though noncontrolling member of the interpretive group, whose role was "to elaborate and develop the students' initial responses to the story and...[to encourage students] to elaborate their own and other students' responses" (1991, p. 402). Ann was not able to play a similar role in her classroom because she was not an integral member of individual book clubs. She clearly recognized the need to encourage students to elaborate and extend their thinking, however. For example, after reading the first entries in the students' Dialogue Journals, she said,

> I've found out, to my dismay, that the reason the journaling took so long the other day is because they summarized the character's story. Ugh! So I've decided that tomorrow I need to give them some direction.... I've been pondering what questions I could pose that would challenge them and force them to go beyond what they have already thought about. I think one will be about the character's future—beyond the novel and perhaps another about the title, or a symbol...it'll be in terms of the character's point of view, though.

Ann plans to use more supplemental materials the next time she teaches this unit. Because of the students' responses to Wong's poem, she is convinced that using these materials will help readers to recognize the author's point of view; how novels represent particular cultural groups; how readers' attitudes and beliefs are affected by what they read; and that cultural groups, including their own, have differing values and norms. On the Post-Unit Survey, only 60% of Ann's students recognized that they had learned about cultures from their novels. Students need to become aware of the power of stories. They need to become more critical as readers unless we want them to absorb information without being aware that they are doing so. Ann recognized that her students' Book Club Organizers and Dialogue Journals were not well done. As a consequence, the resulting book club projects—the activity through which they shared with the rest of the class what they had learned—lacked insight and depth. Not only did readers fail to gain insight about the culture reflected in the book they read, but their lack of critical reading biased what they presented and what they learned about cultural groups other than the one reflected in the books they were reading in their book clubs.

Another researcher, Jordan (1997), also examined how readers respond to culturally diverse texts. She found that students first respond to story and to characters as they have been taught. For most students, this means they respond personally and identify with the text. In order to understand a text, they often supply information either consciously or unconsciously. Perhaps merely because they are young, students have limited knowledge of others. As a result, they often fail to see the intersection between the story world and their schema for understanding the culture. Even when teachers tell students that the text is from a different culture, it has little impact on their reading. When students have trouble reading a text, they perceive the problem to be with themselves as readers or with the author, not with their knowledge of the culture. They make no accommodations in their reading. Instead, they attempt to incorporate what they read into their own worldviews. Jordan maintains that

> it requires a major shift in the way that students read to ask them to explore *differences*—to look for things that they do not understand. If students don't look for differences, they may not ask for information that might help them understand a text, an idea, or another person. (p. 12)

Ann's students were much like this. Information the students obtained from parents, television, and *National Geographic* led to stereotypical generalizations that in turn set up expectations for reading the literature. Having learned generalizations or stereotypes about particular cultures, the students then interpreted situations in literature to prove the generalization. When answering questions about people of color in the real world, the novels were set apart or *re-fenced* (Allport, 1954/1958) and seen as anomalies because they didn't fit the students' perceptions or preconceptions. Although they had been able to experience their characters' worlds and write in their voices, Ann's students failed to see characters' relationships to larger cultural groups. In the same way, students failed to see that they, too, were part of a cultural group with particular norms, values, and biases. Operating within the story world does not mean readers will necessarily transfer what they learn to the real world.

Jordan and Purves (1997) interviewed teachers and secondary school students in an attempt to explore the challenges confronted by teachers and students in relation to reading literature from cultures different from their own. Interviews with the students indicated that they read out of their own experiences and that personalizing the response together with their desire for identification influenced their reading of the texts from other cultures. In Ann's classes, more than 50% of the readers re-created their characters in their

own image by assuming that people of color are unaffected by their ethnicity—
that they have the same opportunities and are as free to act as white people.
Based on student interviews, Jordan and Purves argue that "unless some attempt is made to give students some factual information about the background
culture of texts, then the cycle of one voice, [and the] rejection of unknown
voices, could continue" (p. 17), defeating the main purpose for using multicultural literature. This rejection is not conscious, though. It is more subtle and
insidious because students think they have heard another voice. But the voice
they hear is only their own replayed. Jordan and Purves claim that "before education can be multicultural, there must first be recognition that a dominant
voice persists and that literature is generally taught in that voice" (p. 17).
However, they also found that few teachers involved in the study had the background to teach the texts as cultural artifacts. Even Ann, who sacrificed so
much time and energy to incorporate a multicultural literature unit into an
already overcrowded curriculum, found it difficult to value multicultural literature as highly as the literature with which she is more familiar and feels more
competent teaching. The teachers in the study Jordan and Purves write about
attempted to facilitate understanding through response writing and small-
group discussions, but they didn't provide readers with information about the
cultures. Instead, similar to Ann, they tended to incorporate the texts into an
existing framework of reader response or literary criticism.

Ann and those teachers incorporated the texts into existing frameworks
because learning about cultures takes time and intense study and teachers
don't have these luxuries. Even Ann, who had much more background in the
study of culture than most teachers, struggled to translate her academic learning into classroom teaching. For example, you will note a particularly glaring
error below in the description of *Finding My Voice*. It is common for dominant-
culture readers who may or may not have studied Asian history and culture and
have little day-to-day contact with Asian or Asian American people to group
people of Asian ethnicities together—often as Chinese or Japanese. Ann knew
the difference—in fact, she had a Korean roommate at one time—yet the following excerpt describes an error she included in the form students used to
vote for novels they wished to have included in the unit. None of the students
recognized the error, and Ann didn't catch it until the day the students received
their novels, long after they had read the descriptions. Much to her chagrin,
Ann made a startling discovery:

> Today they had reading time. I started to re-read the novels, too. And I dis-
> covered a horrible mistake! *Finding My Voice* is a Korean American novel, not

Chinese American. I didn't look at it carefully enough, and I had read it last summer. I must have assumed it was Chinese American because the author's last name is Lee...the two are not the same. Yikes!

Even when we know better, stereotypes are insidious and powerful. Although Ann corrected the mistake, she felt strongly that the initial impression would be a lasting one. The short summaries of novels that Ann used to involve the students in selecting the novels to be used in the unit may also have had far-reaching ramifications. Although completely contrary to her intent, Ann may have unintentionally influenced—even predetermined—the way students read by the description of the novels she provided them. Ann focused primarily on the plot but made a strong connection between the culture reflected in the book and the problems created by the dominant culture but faced by the main characters. If Ann had highlighted the cultural strengths of the characters instead, she might have avoided the stereotypical aspects U.S. readers are conditioned to expect. By including cultural strengths in the initial description, she might have made those strengths more salient to students as they read. Contrast the following summaries; the first focuses on the "problem," the second on cultural characteristics.

Journey of the Sparrows

- Story of three kids from El Salvador who illegally come to Chicago in a crate, and who try to make a better life for themselves and their family.

- Contemporary story of two strong, loving sisters from El Salvador who struggle to care for their younger brother and to reunite their family that has been separated because of persecution. Struggling to survive in Chicago, they demonstrate courage and perseverance, determined to save their mother and a younger sister still stranded in Mexico. A close-knit community of other illegal immigrants provides vital help and support in an often unfriendly and hostile environment.

Shabanu

- Story of a teen who grows up in a nomadic family in Pakistan. She faces family problems and an arranged marriage that she doesn't want.

- Set in the Cholistan desert of contemporary Pakistan, Shabanu grows up in a close nomadic family, loving and caring for her family's camels. Her Muslim family permits her more freedom than many young girls. Shabanu constantly writhes, however, against many of the culture's normal expectations, including the expectation that she and her sister accept arranged marriages to ensure the long-term well-being of the extended family.

Scorpions

- Story of a black guy who lives on the streets in New York City. He struggles with family problems, poverty, gangs, and violence.
- With his brother in jail for murder, Jamal struggles to help his mother by earning money to free his brother, previously the leader of a city gang. Jamal and his friend, Tito, must struggle against overwhelming odds, including peer pressure of an inner-city gang, a younger sister, and an antagonistic school principal. Although separated, they survive because of their commitment to each other and the support of a strong mother and grandmother.

Ann's dismay at the end of the unit may be due in part to the expectations students had about the stories before they read them. She said,

> [They] needed more help than I was able to give them to go beyond the factual events of the novel to think about what their significance might be. Because they were unable to do that well, they were unable to communicate adequately what they were supposed to to their peers.

Enciso (1997) writes that teachers need to learn what will encourage children to explore their own and their peers' ideas about difference and to recognize and question the images and the ideologies that appear in literature. As a beginning point, Enciso suggests struggling with questions relating to audience and sociohistorical attitudes and practices. Citing research by Dyson (1993) and Lensmire (1994) that confirm such effects in writing process classrooms, Enciso posits that "if we choose *not* to explore these questions with children...all of the negotiations of the meaning of difference will be left to those children whose cultural references and perspectives are most understood and valued within the classroom" (p. 38). In Ann's classes, the readers whose voices predominated in the book clubs dictated the meaning of difference by assuming the authority role previously filled by the teacher.

Personal and Systemic Racism

In her journal, Ann reflected that "it is very difficult to teach [students] about grayness when they are in such a black and white stage in their thinking and development." Response to literature involves empathizing with characters and then connecting that to one's own experience and one's own position in the real world, but it also involves constructing alternative versions of reality and self. According to Beach (1997), awareness of "how one's own ideological stance shapes the meaning of one's experience with literature" (p. 83) is central to constructing such alternatives. To determine how readers' ideologies affected their reading, Beach examined how students from three high schools—two suburban and primarily white high schools and one urban high school with a high percentage of students of color—responded to advertising. He found that students in the two suburban schools tended to approach reading with the schema that prejudice is an individual characteristic. Students in the urban school, on the other hand, tended to read with a schema that racism is institutionalized. He concluded that students who benefit from systems that confer power, privilege, and economic power based on race tend to be unaware of these systemic advantages because the white perspective is presented as the norm. Beach's findings support his conclusions from an earlier study examining students' responses to ads and to stories (Beach & Freedman, 1992):

> To foster critical response to the media [including stories], educators need to do more than have students analyze the logical fallacies in advertising claims. They need to help students recognize that their responses to the media are cultural practices shaped by ideological forces. Because many adolescents live in cultural cocoons—homogeneous, middle- or working-class communities whose schools reflect community values—this is a challenging task. Just as fish may not know they are swimming in water, so adolescents may not recognize their lives are shaped by cultural values without exposure to alternative values. (p. 183)

In *Through Whose Eyes? Exploring Racism: Reader, Text, and Context*, Naidoo (1992), author of several young adult novels, tells the story of the year she spent reading and discussing literature with a class of affluent, white 11- to 16-year-old high school students in a church school. Using a variety of reader response strategies together with literature that strongly indicts racism, she attempted to "investigate the potential for certain works of literature...to extend white students' empathies; to challenge ethnocentric and racist assumptions and concepts; and to develop critical thinking about the nature of [British] society" (p. 21). In addition to identifying students' personal frames of reference, she wanted to determine whether reading, discussion, and specific interventions would cause a shift in readers' concepts and assumptions. She also hoped to determine whether students' responses would reveal a common "filter," or construct, related to race (p. 21).

In many ways, my findings about Ann's students are congruent with those of Naidoo. Naidoo found that, overall, students liked the books they read just as Ann's readers did. But Naidoo found clear limits to empathy. Many students, particularly boys, who expressed empathy with characters who were targets of racism, also were willing to exonerate the perpetrators. This, too, appears quite congruent with the responses on the Post-Unit Survey. Ann's students gave no evidence of carry-over of empathy from the stories to the real world. Purves (1993) argues,

> In literature programs our students are not simply reading texts, they are reading writers.... They also need to acknowledge themselves as readers with prejudices, ignorance, and beliefs that impinge on their readings and interpretations.... They are learning to interpret themselves as readers as well as to interpret the authors as writers. They are members of a culture with the habits of that culture engaged in reading the work of inhabitants of other cultures. (p. 359)

Even when readers empathize with characters they perceive as "other," Naidoo (1992) found that literature, including literature written from a strongly antiracist perspective, is not enough by itself to change the boundaries of "otherness." She concludes that even strong antiracist literature is unlikely "to challenge racist assumptions except for those in some way already open and ready to hear" (p. 138). Naidoo suggests that readers are more likely to respond by designating events as exceptions or anomalies. If they could see the story or character as an exception, they didn't have to change their thinking about the cultural group. Although Naidoo did find instances of students moving beyond empathy to some kind of reconstruction of their frames of reference, she questioned whether the changes would be sufficient to affect the students' everyday lives or whether they would become merely, as she quotes Eagleton (1985), "sensitive...about nothing in particular" (p. 139). However, she argues that students who tend to be open "need exposure to other voices and other ways of seeing, just as much as those who tend towards being closed and intolerant" (p. 140), because the open ones have the most chance of recognizing that their views of race have been learned and can be changed.

Naidoo's students demonstrated strong feelings against racism both before and after the course, but, like the suburban school students in Beach's study, their concept of racism remained limited to personal attitudes, behaviors, and relationships. Students didn't recognize that social structures solidify and perpetuate such personal biases on a societal level. They seemed willing to see racism as something "out there," but it was much more difficult and quite disturbing for students to see racism in themselves or their immediate groups. At ages 14 and 15, they were just beginning to recognize that individuals are influenced by and contribute to the social and historical context of which they are a part. Naidoo concludes that "in addressing racism with white students, one is challenging them not only to extend their range of empathy but to question their frames of reference and thus elements of their own identities" (p. 146). This is no easy task nor is it a comfortable one.

In Naidoo's study, the regular classroom teacher was supportive of the research project as it began but became increasingly antagonistic. Naidoo describes him as "predominantly didactic, traditionally formal, and by his own acknowledgment disciplinarian" (p. 146). Naidoo argues that, instead, an ethos of tolerance, trust, respect, equality, and interdependence is necessary if students are to be open-minded enough "to extend their range of empathy...question their frames of reference and thus elements of their own identities" (p. 146). Although Ann appeared to share some of the characteristics Naidoo attributes to the teacher in her study, particularly that of being a benevolent authority, she recognized these characteristics in her teaching and, of her own volition, attempted to modify them and to incorporate those characteristics that Naidoo insisted are needed. Naidoo found that the role of the teacher was a difficult one of providing both support and challenge. Unless the climate is trusting and supportive, students become defensive. Unless they are challenged, there can't be change. If students are to become aware that racism goes beyond the personal or behavioral level, they need models. They need teachers willing to verbalize their own struggles to recognize the lenses through which they see the world and who question their own knowledge and how it has been shaped by those lenses. She posits that recognizing one's inadequacy must lead teachers to acknowledge themselves as co-learners and concludes that

> the teacher is an essential element within her or his own pedagogical framework. To help create trust leading to self-esteem, tolerance leading to openmindedness and collaboration leading to a respect for equality, the teacher has to practise all those qualities. (pp. 146–147)

The Critical Role of the Teacher

The next time Ann teaches a multicultural unit, she plans to help students read novels not just as entertaining stories but with a more critical eye about how the novels represent cultural groups, about how their own attitudes and beliefs are affected by what they read, and with more respect for different cultural norms. To do this, Ann knows she will have to spend much more time, prior to reading the novels, talking with students and examining questions of culture, cultural dominance, stereotypes, power differences between cultural groups, cultural privilege, and cultural authenticity in a collaborative atmosphere. Because the reading and the book clubs with their final projects resulted in both students and teacher being busy and distracted, next time she plans to spend more time focusing on "how to think differently, how to question the world, and how to make inferences" before initiating the book clubs. Including more materials like poetry and essays that would increase students' exposure to different perspectives and literary forms would help achieve this goal. She also will change projects from those that have the potential for being quick and easy (such as talk shows and news broadcasts) to those that would encourage depth of perception, thoroughness, and thoughtfulness (perhaps a movie or sit-com). To discourage the stereotypical book report mind-set, Ann anticipates assigning a similar project about a novel earlier in the year, thus developing a model that would lend itself more easily to the reflection of abstract content. She would also structure the Dialogue Journal differently so that it would result in students delving more deeply into issues from the character's perspective rather than merely summarizing the events of the novel. She is considering structuring it like her current thinkbooks where the journal writer gets three topics or questions per week to write about and the responder pushes the journal writer to think more deeply. Although she recognizes that her questions will be couched in dominant-culture ways of thinking, she hopes to move with her students to the point of asking, If this character were asking the questions, what would they be? Her goal will be to recognize that each culture has its unique way of addressing the universal aspects of human experience.

The need to incorporate focused discussion emerges as one of the strongest and most consistent themes throughout this book. Van Dyke (1997) offers a concise summary of existing research:

> One thing is clear from the research which has attempted to examine the potential use of literature to modify attitudes and beliefs. The power of discussion cannot be ignored. Although in a few instances change was noted with just reading the texts, when discussion occurred an often greater change was indicated. (p. 16)

Ann, too, recognized the need to incorporate substantially more discussion when students read multicultural literature and acknowledged the importance of keeping the discussion focused. In addition to honoring individual response, the discussion must involve both teachers and students in talking about values and beliefs and how these are lived out. Differences and similarities must be recognized, and otherness must be discussed. Students must be challenged to consider the effects of systems that favor one cultural group over another. Seeing characters as individuals rather than members of cultural groups permitted Ann's students to see individual characters as exceptions to the group and thus permitted these readers to maintain their initial schema for understanding the real world. Seeing both the characters and themselves as individuals rather than as part of societal or cultural groups also meant that students perceived racism as individual acts and thus random rather than part of systemic bias. But racism means that individuals who share characteristics preferred in a particular society have greater opportunities and more freedoms than those who do not have those characteristics. It means that preferred groups have economic and social advantages because the systems that are in place are designed to confer those privileges automatically. For example, it is easy to find flesh-colored bandages or makeup, but the flesh color is white. And when authorities seek terrorists European Americans are seldom detained. Students will begin to recognize the real meaning of racism only when they recognize that individuals are part of larger cultural groups and that particular groups have more or less power in particular societies.

Most systems in the United States advantage whites merely because of skin color, not because of some personal merit (McIntosh, 1989). Those who are white implicitly participate in and benefit from systemic racism. Retaining such economic and social advantages depends on the ability of whites to convince themselves that they have earned their advantage—that opportunities are equally available to anyone who works hard enough. It is in their favor to maintain that all people are the same. Such thinking preserves the existing power differential. Only people of the dominant culture, those who benefit from this system of unearned advantage, promote this argument. Until dominant-culture readers are able to accept the reality that people are perceived differently within particular systems and that those systems have built-in mechanisms to automatically confer that power on members of particular groups, they will continue to re-create characters in their own images. To do otherwise means recognizing the discrepancy between themselves and others, recognizing that our society is not an equitable one, and recognizing that people with power are the ones who must act to change the systems. It means that readers must confront their own racism. As Ann put it,

It's easy for the students and the teacher to wrap themselves in a warm blanket of "aren't we good people because we're learning about these other people" and, thus, never deal with the crucial issue of "how did these 'other' people get to be 'other' anyway?"

CHAPTER 5

What It All Means
and What We Can Do

> *The teacher's relationship with the students and helping them to expand their thinking are the most important goals. That is more important than getting them to believe that racism is wrong. Each of us is racist to some degree or another; and if we reject students because they do not think like we do, we are reinforcing their right to reject the particular culture we want them to understand and accept. If changing students' thinking to be more like yours is more important to you than challenging and expanding their thinking, you should not teach multicultural literature. (Ann)*

The purpose of this book has been to help teachers teach multicultural literature more effectively by telling the story of one teacher and one classroom as they read multicultural literature together. By determining whether the students met their teacher's goals, my goal was to learn about readers, their response to literature, and their learning about culture. As I examined what happened when 123 dominant-culture students read literature about cultures different from their own, I found myself questioning and challenging commonly accepted assumptions. I have shared my questions with you and have attempted to shed light on those questions by talking about the findings of other researchers.

The following is a brief summary of what I've talked about in the previous pages and some suggestions about how teachers can encourage readers to "value all peoples, accept differences as a natural aspect of human societies, and even celebrate cultural pluralism as a desirable feature of the world in which they live" (Bishop, 1997, pp. vii–viii) within the context of aesthetic response.

Did the Readers Enjoy Multicultural Literature?

Yes. Readers of all abilities enjoyed the multicultural texts they read during this unit. Ann reflects their excitement in her journal. Overall, there was clearly a move from negative or neutral feelings about reading novels to positive feelings about reading the novels used in the unit. It is especially interesting that 13 of 21 students, who indicated before the unit that either they didn't like to read, had trouble reading, or didn't like reading school-assigned material, felt positively about reading their books.

Even though the number willing to read about characters different from themselves did not increase after the unit, neither did it decrease. After the unit, significantly more students still said they would choose to read a multicultural novel again ($p < .0001$). This result isn't really surprising given Ann's commitment to having her students enjoy and understand multicultural novels. She knew that most students in her classes were not avid readers. She also knew that students react more positively to texts that they have a part in choosing, so she involved them in the selection process in two ways: First, they helped select the six novels to be used in the unit; second, they identified and got to read one of their top three choices.

Implications for the Classroom

- Be committed to incorporating multicultural literature into your curricula.
- Place a high priority on getting readers engaged with their reading.
- Involve students in book selection.
- Give readers some choice in which books they read.

Did Readers Participate in an Aesthetic Transaction?

Yes. Ann's students participated in what Rosenblatt (1985) calls "another's vision" by living through "ideas, sensations, images, tensions" as they created their "poem[s]" (p. 103). Ninety-three percent of Ann's students clearly operated within the story world when they wrote in their Dialogue Journals from a character's perspective. When Ann evaluated the unit, she realized that she received few complaints about the amount of work—even the kind of work the students generally disliked. She concluded that,

Undoubtedly, the most positive part of the unit was the enjoyment the students derived from the novels. I had been led to believe by some colleagues that students generally do not like multicultural fiction, and I did not find that to be the case at all. Several students asked me personally for recommendations of other books "like this one."... This pleases me both because I wanted them to like reading about people from a different cultural background than their own and because I want them to like reading.

Other researchers have also found that ethnicity is not a key component of aesthetic response. Young people, regardless of their ethnicity, like good stories regardless of the ethnicity of the characters. Remember Altieri's (1996) research, for example: After hearing stories reflecting different cultural groups, written responses of fifth and seventh graders of different cultures indicated that "overall the level of aesthetic involvement was not significantly influenced by the ethnicity of student or culture portrayed in the story" (p. 237).

In observing his middle school students, Wilhelm (1997) found that "multicultural literature, in particular, help[ed] students to enter other perspectives" (p. 35). Wilhelm's thrust is that many less proficient readers have never been taught "how to evoke and enter a secondary world" (p. 99). One technique he found useful in helping readers to re-create a secondary world was story drama, which requires readers to respond to a situation or conflict from a character's point of view. Perhaps the Dialogue Journal assignment served a similar purpose for Ann's students by helping them enter the world of their stories. If this made their reading more satisfying, it may have resulted in less resistance by the students toward their daily assignments.

Another important aspect of Wilhelm's study is that of the democratic classroom. Although Wilhelm's students did not appear to interact as equals at the beginning of the year, he indicates that they did so by the end of the study. He attributes this to his shift in focus from having one correct understanding or interpretation of the text to the validity of individual responses, each enriched by the responses of others. Such equality is a unique situation and not present in all classrooms (see, for example, Lensmire, 1994). Whenever one voice or one group becomes privileged by having a more valid "answer" than another, a hierarchy is established. So, when the teacher is the interpretive authority—even a benevolent authority—the classroom becomes an autocracy. This was probably true in Ann's classroom. But during this unit, Ann changed her normal pattern of instruction to follow what she had been taught was best practice. She vacated the position of interpretive authority, and when she did so, a void was created. Rather than resulting in a more democratic classroom, the void was merely filled by another autocratic voice, that of the dominant voice(s) in the book clubs. When some children are permitted to dominate the literature classroom, their voices and their ideas are reinforced as being more valid, even if by default. When an authoritative voice, whether the teacher's or that of vocal students, dominates the literary conversation, keeping others out, it prevents students from "understanding other perspectives and [developing] a personal sense of agency in the world" (Wilhelm, 1997, p. 152). The very reason teachers use multicultural literature in the first place is undermined.

Implications for the Classroom

- Assume that your students will like multicultural books. The findings of this study provide overwhelming evidence that they will, so talk, act, and teach accordingly. Select well-written literature, preferably stories recommended by reviews from the culture in the book.

- Help readers re-create a story world. Involve students in the visual arts and drama. Provide opportunities to discuss alternative perspectives. Let students teach one another how they read.

- Strive for a more democratic classroom: Share the interpretive role, but do not permit a student to dominate the literary conversation in large-group discussions or literature circles.

- Avoid favoring one personal response over others. Insist that all readers provide support for their interpretations, either from the text or other relevant material.

- Refrain from providing *the* definitive interpretation no matter how convinced you are about how the text must be read.

- Build on students' personal responses to literature: Help readers "grow meaning" by comparing their personal responses with the written text and with the understanding of others. Encourage them—even insist that they defend their readings, if they can, from the written text.

Did the Readers Increase Their Understanding of Others?

No—not about people in the real world, but perhaps they did increase their understanding about characters in the stories. When writing about their books, 75% of readers appeared to grasp what it means to be part of a group with unique customs, characteristics, and language patterns that inevitably result in a unique "worldview or culture or sensibility" (Sims, 1982, p. 13). However, only 24% of readers did so when they left the realm of literature and completed their Post-Unit Surveys about "people." This same pattern emerged in relation to norms and values of other cultures, including matters pertaining to family, age, gender, and religion: The cultural understanding students demonstrated when writing specifically about their books did not transfer to their answers about people or groups in the real world. Perhaps because they had little or no understanding of how ethnicity and ethnic attitudes have been constructed historically, they recognized difference but not privilege. They saw no connection between themselves and their lives and colonialism, capitalism, or the relationship between dominant and nondominant groups in their society. In fact, 50% of the students considered people of color to be "other," and 32% of students considered themselves to be people of good will—sympathizing, defending, and justifying. Only 6% of students saw people from nondominant cultures as equal to people of the dominant culture.

Perhaps the most interesting findings of the study are the readers' perceptions of the nondominant characters in the books they read. When reading their books, more than 50% of students were blind to consequences of color. They assumed that characters from nondominant cultures were as free to act and to make decisions, as they, themselves, were. For example, many readers were righteously indignant when Maria's boss attempted to molest her in *Journey of the Sparrows*. But they felt that Maria, an illegal immigrant from El Salvador, should have quit her job as they would have done. They gave little evidence of recognizing that, for Maria and her family, the consequences were dire and life threatening. Maria was not free, in the way they were, to make that choice. Almost 30% of students, however, did recognize that nondominant characters lived between two worlds. Many realized that Danny in *Shadow of the Dragon* lived in the world of U.S. teenagers when he was with his peers but faced a totally different set of responsibilities at home where he was the oldest son, responsible for the behavior of his siblings.

By applying the work of Donald Davidson (1984, 1986) to artistic interpretation, Dasenbrock (1992) developed an interesting theory about how readers create a secondary world different from their own. Using Davidson's terms, the theory posits that each person has a worldview, a set of personal constructs, a "prior theory" (p. 40). When meeting a person about whom we know nothing, we employ our "prior theory." However, we also employ what Davidson calls "interpretive charity" (p. 40), thus assuming that the person thinks, means, and sees things exactly as we do. But because this never works—even if we speak the same language—we soon recognize discrepancies between our understanding and that of the person with whom we are trying to communicate. Dasenbrock assumes readers will recognize such discrepancy in their reading of written texts also. When they recognize the points at which their own worldview diverges from that of the text, he says that readers will use a "passing theory" (p. 41). Using this passing theory as a basis, we collect information and continue to make adjustments in our prior theory about a person until we understand the difference between our way of seeing things and the other person's meanings and beliefs. This difference may be merely a different way of using words but is more likely to indicate a different set of beliefs. Dasenbrock sees his theory as an alternative to both author-centered and reader response theories of literary understanding. Invoking Davidson, he says, "we continue to adjust our interpretations until we think they are true, until we stop having to adjust them because of the anomalies we perceive" (p. 42).

If Dasenbrock's theory is accurate, it means that the more literature people read that counters their existing stereotypes about people of cultures different from their own, the more they will be called on to adjust those stereotypes. This is certainly strong support for increasing the amount of multicultural literature students read. It is important to remember, however, that Dasenbrock's passing theory never comes into play for reluctant readers who are unable to enter the story in the first place. And, even for good readers, it appears that such a theory may help explain what readers do, but does not address to what extent particular readers will better understand the "other," will see the "other" as an anomaly within the "foreign" culture, or will re-create the "other" in the image of the reader.

The perceptions that Ann's students had about people of cultures different from their own are complicated by another finding: When all written work was considered, 88% of readers did *not* recognize that Korean Americans, Vietnamese Americans, or Chinese Americans were U.S. citizens, nor were African Americans or Latina/Latino peoples "American" in the same way the readers were.

Implications for the Classroom

- Encourage students to read many books written by authors from cultures other than their own.
- Discourage students from identifying with characters when this really means "re-creating" characters in their own images. Insist that they recognize the differences between themselves and the characters.

- Stimulate discussion of multicultural literature. Provide opportunities for students to express their opinions. Seek out opinions that differ from one another. Offer your own perspective. Unless the teacher takes an active role, children whose voices dominate in the classroom will control the negotiations about the meaning of difference.

- Consider the author a member of the conversation. Consider the author's perspective, cultural affiliation, norms, and values, but do not permit the author to dominate the discussion.

- Learn together about differing worldviews. Learn to recognize cultural markers and the meanings attached to them. Learn how those cultural specifics play out in the lives of real people.

- Help students to understand the lives of people in parallel cultures by focusing on the relationships within the story rather than focusing only on events in the plot.

- Remember that operating within a story world does not mean that readers will necessarily transfer what they learn to the real world. Recognize and confront readers' tendency to consider stories of nondominant characters as anomalies and, therefore, not related to the real world as they know it.

- Use literary terms whenever discussing literature. Characters are not real people. Stories are not reality although they are often related to reality.

- Remind readers that characters may not have the same opportunities within existing systems as do dominant-culture characters or dominant-culture readers. Discuss the reality of living in the United States as a member of a nondominant culture.

- Recognize that individuals are unique but that they are also part of cultural groups, and membership in those groups often determines their opportunities or lack of opportunities.

- Provide opportunities for students to interact personally with people of various cultural backgrounds. Face-to-face contact is invaluable. Pen pals are available on the Web. Authentic films and videos demonstrate what it means to grow up as a member of a nondominant culture.

- Make use of Internet resources. Many authors, professional organizations, and cultural groups have websites. Look for resources that reflect an "insider's" perspective. For example, http://www.oyate.org

critiques books to determine their accuracy in reflecting specific Native American nations. In addition to identifying what is inaccurate or offensive, the reviews often highlight accurate information contained in the book.

- Learn the requirements of U.S. citizenship. Begin by going to the website for U.S.A. Immigration Services (http://www.usais.org). Additional information can be found in encyclopedias, civics books, and tradebooks.

- Learn the rights that belong to *all* U.S. citizens. Begin with the U.S. Constitution and the Bill of Rights. Much information is available on the Internet. The U.S. Government Printing Office has a website called Ben's Guide for Kids to U.S. Government (http://bensguide.gpo.gov). This site includes resources and links to other sites for parents. Additional resources are available through school and local libraries.

- Learn what rights belong to all people whether citizens or not. A good place to begin is the United Nations website (http://www.un.org). Click on Human Rights and be sure to read the United Nations Universal Declaration of Human Rights.

- Revisit the idea that all U.S. citizens, except Native Americans, are descended from immigrants.

- Distinguish literature about U.S. citizens from literature about people outside the United States.

- Read literature about immigrants and literature about long-term citizens at different times and discuss how the struggles of these groups differ.

Did Readers Grow in Their Understanding of Themselves or Their Cultural Values?

No. Although students were specifically asked in the Book Club Organizer to compare the character's world and its values to their own, few gave evidence of any increase in understanding of themselves or their own world. To the extent that they recognized that they belonged to a particular culture with particular norms and values, they accepted those norms and values as givens. The students did not appear to recognize that others might see the world differently. Although they frequently talked about the way characters and people from other cultures thought and acted, students' writing indicated that they did not recognize that they were implicitly comparing the norms and values of other cultures to their own. Instead, readers re-created characters in their own images, each assuming that his or her own view of the world was *the* view rather than recognizing it as one of many. Like readers who talk face-to-face, the students

> [assumed] a common representation or world view from the start…[and] in the end, they…fitted the story into their world view, assimilated it…. In a very real sense, they…[had] *given it* the meaning which it will have for them. (Applebee, 1978, p. 7)

Implications for the Classroom

- Bring your own norms and values to conscious awareness. Students recognize teachers' values whether teachers acknowledge them or not. Recognizing and discussing your norms and values and their impact on your thinking and decision-making will help students recognize and begin to identify the norms and values that guide their thoughts and actions.

- Make visible the cultural markers of the dominant culture. Cultures have characteristics that are shared to some extent by members of the group. The dominant culture (white, male, Anglo-Saxon) is often described as individualistic, self-focused, and competitive as opposed to being group-oriented, other-directed, and cooperative. Misunderstood, these generalizations often become stereotypes, but understood within the context of the culture, they can help reveal the motivations, actions, and reactions of characters and people. Cultural markers of the dominant culture are often highlighted in books and articles comparing the dominant culture and its literature to other cultures and their literature (see, for example, http://www.oyate.org).

- Recognize that groups to which readers belong—their cultures, their families, their peer groups, their classrooms, their book clubs—exert powerful influence. Most people will strive to maintain their membership in groups that are important to them; it is sometimes easier to change the group than it is to change the individual within the group.

- Do not assume that dominant-culture values are the norm or that what is normal for you is normal for everyone.

- Do not deny differences. Recognize that only people in power choose to maintain that "we" are all the same. Only people of the dominant culture talk this way. This way of thinking preserves the power differential. Insisting that "we" are all equal means that those with power do not have to acknowledge their power. Failing to acknowledge the existing power differential reinforces the status quo. However, recognizing the unearned advantage of being white means dominant-culture people cannot continue to ignore the inequality that exists between cultural groups. It means that they will have to act or acknowledge that they are comfortable with things the way they are. People of nondominant cultures know that systems currently in place exclude them from participating equally in the "we" of U.S. society.

- Stimulate discussions that bring students face to face with the present day ramifications of systemic racism. Discuss the values inherent in these systems. Make explicit the range of other possible value positions.

- Learn about and discuss the consequences of actions by dominant-culture systems on people of nondominant cultures.

- Do not use the passive voice when talking about racism. People must take responsibility for their actions or lack of action. The passive voice is often used to avoid taking responsibility. The passive voice says that people of nondominant cultures are discriminated against, but it does not reveal who does the discriminating: People of the dominant culture discriminate against people of nondominant cultures. Sometimes they are not aware they are discriminating, but they receive benefits merely because they are of the dominant culture; sometimes they choose not to recognize those benefits. Sometimes they discriminate by being passive or avoiding responsibility by speaking or writing in the passive voice.

Did the Readers Read Against the Text?

No. The students' writing gave little evidence that they went beyond an aesthetic transaction. However, at one point, the responses of some students in their Dialogue Journals did question the text or the author, but these responses were written in response to a question or suggestion from the teacher. Throughout the existing research on multicultural literature, the role of the teacher appears crucial. Encouraging open dialogue about ethnicity and its implications is vital in all areas of instruction. Even the teacher's assumptions need to be questioned. In Ann's unit, the short summaries of novels that she wrote to involve the students in selecting the novels to be used in the unit probably influenced the way her students read. By recognizing this and discussing it with her students, Ann could have provided a powerful model for them.

Implications for the Classroom

- Value personal response and build on it to develop understanding.
- Challenge readers to examine their responses. Why did they respond as they did? Was there something in the text that triggered a particular response? Was the response a result of an assumption that the reader made? Readers are responsible for meanings they make of a text. They must think critically about what they read and make conscious decisions about how it will influence their understanding. They must grow, broadening and revising their initial responses.
- Discuss various responses. Remember, some are more defensible within the context of the story than others.
- Learn to recognize authors' different perspectives in literature. Recognize that authors differ, their cultural experiences differ, and their cultural loyalties differ. Some write from within a culture, and some write from the outside. Different authors will embed different cultural details in the narrative, the description, the settings, and the dialogue.
- Describe a character's behavior within a cultural context rather than relying on plot summaries filtered through dominant-culture sensibilities.
- Question everything. Begin to challenge your own assumptions. For example, when confronted with the way things are, ask if this is the way things are or if this is the way things are for you; when you like a particular piece of literature, consider whether you like it because it reflects the way you think about the world; when grappling with facts, consider who is presenting the facts and why. An effective way to begin this process is to compare two accounts of history, one written by a dominant-culture historian, the other written by a historian of a non-dominant culture in the United States.
- Recognize that all readings are political. When our reading reflects the norms and values of our culture, it is much more difficult to recognize politicalness. If and when we re-create stories to reflect our own lives, we impose our culture on the story. We become, in effect, colonizers.

Did the Readers Change?

Perhaps a bit. Students' learning about the nondominant culture reflected in the book they read tended to be slightly more realistic in 65% of the Book Club

Organizers but was primarily stereotypical in 32%. Students tended toward a more realistic understanding in 57% of the Dialogue Journals but were primarily stereotypical in 32% of the Dialogue Journals. The interrater reliability was .84 and .81, respectively, indicating a highly reliable finding. It is imperative, however, to understand that *realistic* was defined in this study as *any* movement toward accuracy, even if only a very small movement about one group.

Although they were often very stereotypical, 50% of students appeared either to be more accurate—or at least more positive—about nondominant cultures after the unit. The other 50% did not appear to change at all. Although about 40% of students were either negative or paternalistically stereotypical at the end of the unit, the good news is that none appeared to have become more negative.

Implications for the Classroom

- Realize that change comes slowly.
- Acknowledge, celebrate, and encourage readers when they begin to question their assumptions.
- Introduce and discuss oral and written materials that reflect an accurate image of nondominant people in particular cultures.
- Identify and discuss stereotypes of the dominant and nondominant cultures. Stereotypes are often grounded in reality but they always serve the interests of a particular group.
- Help students become acquainted with people of nondominant cultures. Personal contact is the most effective but video, film, audiotapes, and other media can help.
- Interact with people who belong to groups other than dominant cultures and are aware of their positions in their society. Listen to them. Interview them.

Relation Among Aesthetic Transaction, Understanding, and Evaluation

This study indicates that the relationship between readers' aesthetic response and cultural understanding was highly significant ($r = .59$, $p < .0001$), which is consistent with previous research. For example, Cox and Many (1992) report that their research supports Rosenblatt's contention that readers must first participate in personal response if they are to develop understanding that reflects real knowing. They write, "our studies have...indicated that the relationship between stance and understanding is fairly consistent across texts...when readers focused on the lived-through experience of most stories, their reported responses were consistently richer in understanding" (p. 118). For Ann's students, too, there was a relationship between aesthetic response and understanding. Besides that, their understanding was significantly related to their CTBS total scale score for reading, language, and math (r = 46, p < .0001) and to the English grade they earned from Ann at the end of the year. More interesting and perhaps most important, however, is that the relationship between the reader's degree of understanding and Ann's grade is significantly greater than the relationship between the reader's understanding and his or her test score (p < .012).

Implications for the Classroom

- Involve your students in selecting the literature to be read.

- Encourage readers to participate in a virtual experience of the story. Do everything in your power to help this happen. Learning that grows out of response results in understanding.

- Expect and accept readings that diverge from the text, but use them to stimulate learning. Insist that readers defend their reading within the parameters of the text.

- Expect readers to project their norms and values on the characters in the text. Use this to stimulate learning about the norms and values of dominant and nondominant cultures and about the systemic bias in language as well as in other systems.

- Introduce dissonance into discussions. Never be satisfied with simplistic answers or ones that dismiss complex questions with quick resolutions.

- Trust yourself to know, like Ann did, what your readers are learning.

The Unit in the Context of Multicultural Education

Before concluding, I want to discuss Ann's unit within the context of a broader view of multicultural education. You may be familiar with the writings of authors in the field of multicultural education like James Banks and Sonia Nieto. Banks (2002) identifies four approaches to curriculum reform: the contributions approach, the additive approach, the transformation approach, and the social action approach. The contributions approach is characterized by including in the curriculum such things as holidays and celebrations. The additive approach goes beyond contributions to incorporate cultural content, but it does not change the basic structure of the curriculum. According to Banks, the transformation approach is fundamentally different from the first two because

> it changes the canon, paradigms, and basic assumptions of the curriculum and enables students to view concepts, issues, themes, and problems from different perspectives and points of view.... [Students] are given the opportunity to formulate and justify their own versions of events and situations. Important aims of the transformation approach are to teach students to think critically and to develop the skills to formulate, document, and justify their conclusions and generalizations. (p. 31)

The social action approach extends the transformation curriculum by enabling students to act personally and collectively on their learning.

It seems to me that Banks would describe Ann's approach to curriculum as a transformation approach. However, Ann's actions in transforming her curriculum would have to be described as social action. That is, by designing and teaching this unit, Ann has acted on what she had learned. By asking her students to think critically and to view life from a perspective different from their own, Ann acted to challenge her students to act differently. It's interesting to speculate on what other kinds of things Ann might incorporate into her curriculum as she moves forward.

To extend her commitment to multiculturalism, Ann might begin next year by extending her attempts to get her readers engaged with their reading. One of three primary goals for her multicultural literature unit was for students to enjoy reading and understanding a novel. Perhaps she could involve students in book selection for all her units. She might provide readers with some choice in which books they read, and she might incorporate books by authors from nondominant cultures throughout the units she teaches rather than reading them only during a multicultural unit.

She might also rethink her role as the interpretive authority in the classroom. One of Ann's cherished goals was to help her students think critically, especially understanding multiple points of view. This goal wasn't limited to the multicultural literature unit. Teachers, by virtue of age and education, know and understand things that students don't, and I am not suggesting that teachers abdicate their responsibility; however, the line between a benevolent authority and a democratic leader is a fine one. Students often see things in literature that teachers don't. Listening to students, valuing their responses, and engaging in honest discussion models respect for multiple points of view. But this can be merely a technique. Teachers honestly must be willing to change, and they must demonstrate this willingness by listening intently and giving serious consideration to alternative perspectives by debating—maybe even aloud—the pros and cons of those perspectives.

In addition to demonstrating the search for multiple perspectives in a multicultural unit, Ann might choose to focus, from the beginning of the school year, on the broad topic of perspective in all the literature her students read. Focusing on perspective, even in the required canon, would help readers consider multiple views of reality in all their reading: Why do characters act as they do? What influences an author? How does the reader respond and why does he or she respond that way? Do authors and readers share similar views of the world? How do gender, social status, language, race, ethnicity, religion, and sexual preference affect the characters? The author? The reader? The teacher? What are the most common genres of literature written by authors of particular cultures?

One of the ways I introduce this idea in my university classes is to begin the discussion by asking students to imagine what characteristics they would look for in an author if they wanted to know more about premenstrual syndrome (PMS). Certainly, not all teachers will want to ask about PMS in the classroom, but you could devise a similar question appropriate for your own context. Most students in my classes are female and the immediate response is uproarious laughter. The few males in the class are usually silent. I ask, "Would you want to read a book by a woman with PMS? A woman without PMS? A doctor? Or, a man who lives with a woman who has PMS?" At this point, everyone laughs, especially the young men. Perceptive students ask, "Is the doctor a woman?" Regardless of their responses, the answer is always that the characteristics you would look for depend on what you want to know. And students recognize that, although most of them had assumed at the beginning that they would want to read a book by a woman with PMS, other perspectives would be better if they wanted to understand it in other ways. And I remind them, if they want to know what it feels like to suffer from PMS, they will need to read many books written by different women with PMS. No one book or author can portray the experience of an entire group of people.

This exercise does something else, too. It tends to bring together the class into a unified whole; it helps me create what Banks (2002) refers to as a "caring community" (p. 108). The women in my classes realize that I am thoughtful and that perhaps they can learn from me. The men realize that I recognize the rights of the nondominant culture—women in the world as it exists today and men in my classroom. This helps bring us together as a group without insiders or outsiders. This becomes especially important because opening ourselves to learn from one another involves trust and vulnerability.

I have been thinking and teaching about diversity for more than 20 years. One of the most important things I have learned during that time is how very much I don't know. I share with my students that my goal for the class is for each of us to learn more than we already know now about perspectives in literature, in this case, literature written by people of nondominant cultures in the United States. The only way that can happen, however, is for us to be able to share with one another what we don't know. This is, perhaps, the most difficult thing we do in class. Teachers are supposed to know the answers; at least, that's the stereotype. But of course, no one can know everything. Still, some people would like others to believe they can. Rather than trying to be knowledge dispensers, teachers need to be master learners, and the best teachers teach others how to learn. However, many students and their parents may not see teaching that way. You will have to model a real teacher for them, and that is not easy—to be a learner when the stereotype says you should be a dispenser of information.

It is difficult to acknowledge that there are very simple things that we don't know. It is more difficult to realize that the way we think may be stereotypical, or discriminatory, or even racist. It is difficult for us as teachers, and it is difficult for students. But when I begin to list questions for which I want answers, my students begin to relax. They are always surprised that my questions (at least at the beginning) are concrete, not abstract, theoretical, or ethereal. Yet, they also are relieved. It doesn't take long for us to generate a long list of what we're supposed to know but don't, as well as things we aren't supposed to know but do: Why are African Americans musically and athletically superior, or are they? Do Native Americans prefer the term *Native American*, or *Indian*, or something else? Are Puerto Ricans U.S. citizens? Why are Chinese Americans so reserved, or are they? Why are so many African Americans on welfare, or are they? Why are so many African American males in prison? (I recommend Randall Robinson's [2002] *The Reckoning* for a powerful exploration of this last question.)

Many of these questions relate to stereotypes, which are complicated because they appear to have some basis in reality. That reality, however, has been altered to serve the purposes of the person or group doing the stereotyping. Stereotypes may be either positive or negative, but they often serve to consolidate power for those who already have it. That's why, for example, the stereotype of the happy slave was so attractive. Many of Ann's students thought that any negative feelings or opinions they had about a culture were stereotypes, but any positive feelings or opinions were realistic. One of the dangers of challenging existing stereotypes is that we will simply replace one stereotype with another, and positive stereotypes are no less stereotypical than negatives ones. As I mentioned at the beginning of this book, most of the students I teach are dominant-culture readers. One of the ways we begin talking about multicultural literature is to generate a list of our own stereotypes of groups different from us. Last year, as we evaluated what had gone well in our class and what we could have done more effectively, students suggested that we should have started with stereotypes of white people. They felt it would have helped them to recognize stereotypes of themselves in the literature, which would have helped them to recognize when others were being stereotyped.

Reading and sharing literature is, of course, the heart of the literature classroom, however, so is examining what the people from the culture reflected in the literature say about it. Perhaps if Ann had asked her students to read critiques and discussions about their books written by "insiders," they would have been less inclined to re-create the characters in their own images. Perhaps they would have learned more about themselves and their own cultural norms and values. Perhaps what they learned about literature would have transferred to what they knew about real life. Because readers are often "outsiders" to the cultures they are reading about, inside information is needed in order to understand what is being read. Try this yourself: Go to http://www.oyate.org and read the reviews of a book that they *don't* recommend. Whether you agree with the critiques or not, you will be confronted with a perspective you know little about and assumptions and attitudes you didn't know you had. Listening to insiders often helps readers to read in what Jordan and Purves (1993) refer to as "the spirit of the culture" (p. 2).

Another thing Ann might do is have her students work together, perhaps in book clubs, to search for answers to questions. As they read their books, group members might generate questions from their reading, or they might generate questions implicit in a list of stereotypes generated by the class. Instead of assuming the material in the book is accurate (it often isn't, particularly if the author is a member of the dominant culture), each book club might be charged with determining whether the material is accurate from the perspective of the group reflected in the book. Students can seek answers to questions about the author, the characters, the events, and the setting, including the time, place, norms, and values of the time—anything that will help them and their peers to understand better the literature and the people reflected in it. Does the literature accurately portray the particular group of people it supposedly reflects? Are the details, perspective, tone, theme, relationships, and roles included in the book consistent with researched information written by people of the culture? Each book club could then conduct a workshop designed to help others (including the teacher) to better understand the culture and thus become better able to evaluate how literature reflects that culture.

Students could help choose class books, as Ann had them do, or they could choose their own books based on specific criteria. I would encourage—even require—students to read more than one book. Some will choose to read novels, but I would involve students in reading picture books to complement their novels. Picture books are no longer only for young children, and many fine ones are available, with sophisticated stories and artwork. I suggest that both novels and picture books be written and illustrated by members of the culture reflected in the book, that they be identified as quality literature (you might use critiques in respected review journals or reviews written by professionals who are accepted by the culture reflected in the book, but beware—these two groups are not always the same and do not always agree), that they have been recently published, and that they reflect a variety of characters and experiences. Although group members could read one book in common, they might then each read different books to compare with it. If it is absolutely impossible to obtain actual books, a similar project could be designed using an anthology. Students could even evaluate a variety of anthologies.

Challenge students to find the answers rather than providing answers for them. The result, of course, will be a close look at the pluralistic nature of U.S. society and the unique characteristics and contributions of each culture studied as well as differences within the cultures themselves. You might even challenge students to try to discern how literature written by an author from a particular culture differs from that written by an author not of that culture. Or, have students try to generate from the literature read, as well as from secondary sources, hypotheses pertaining to the characteristics of literature from different cultures. In the end, readers will become better able to recognize literature that portrays cultures realistically, as opposed to stereotypically, and to be able to substantiate their decisions.

The research is the fun part. Because students have great freedom in identifying what they want to research, they also have great enthusiasm. I have found that establishing general guidelines is helpful. I can always change them for particular groups or individual students as the need arises. I distribute the following guidelines, discuss them in class, and then adapt them as necessary:

- Turn in a dated record of your research work for the week, indicating the approximate amount of time you spend on each activity listed.

Although you need to document some work each week, you may arrange the hours to fit your schedule. You need to document a total of 36 hours. (Teachers can tailor this to their classrooms.) Documentation may take the following forms and should be submitted the week you complete the activity, although other arrangements can be made: highlighted copies of articles from journals, books, or websites; written summaries; movie reviews; photos; audiotape recordings; and detailed lists.

- Unless you can convince me otherwise, your research must involve material written or created by people of the culture reflected in your book. I will look for a balance among the following tasks:
  - Read materials written by people of the culture: newspapers, articles from a variety of journals, books about the culture, and published interviews with authors.
  - Seek out and view appropriate media.
  - Become immersed in the art and music of the culture, listen to stories told by storytellers of the culture, or attend speeches and lectures by members of the culture.
  - Visit with, talk with, spend time with, and interview members of the culture.
  - Interview people who may not be members of the culture but who claim to be "experts" about the culture.
- Spend as much time on the Internet as you like, but record only two hours per week.
- Spend a majority of your time on meaningful learning activities—not bookkeeping activities— typing, sorting, and organizing materials have their place but should not take the place of more important learning activities.

Because students have a great range of interests and abilities, working in groups permits them to capitalize on their strengths and learn from the strengths of others (see Phelan, Davidson, & Cao, 1992). I have never had a student who could not find something of interest to research, although some resist having to do the work. It is much easier for them to have a teacher provide the answers or at least assign the topics. Presenting material and being responsible for the accuracy of that material is an awesome task. But, it is more difficult to do in a multicultural workshop because I insist that the material must be written or created by people from the culture being researched and sources must be acknowledged. I find, however, that conducting a workshop is incredibly rewarding for most students, especially if they feel they can teach not only their peers but also their teacher.

During a workshop, members of each group share what they have learned about the culture and explain how that learning enriches their understanding of the literature of that group. They might share music, art, food, maps, audio or video recordings, or films they have discovered—whatever they think might help others to understand the culture and, therefore, the literature that comes from it. Groups might choose to be graded as a group or individually. You might require the groups to include particular elements in their workshops. For example, I usually insist that each workshop include the following first four activities to help others gain a better understanding of a cultural group reflected in literature. I also ask each group to select and complete other activities they think will be helpful to other readers. Finally, each group must provide time for peers to respond and ask questions.

- Present an overview of the nondominant culture's history in the United States, with a focus on events that the group feels were formative in the history.
- Invite a speaker(s) from the nondominant culture to talk to the class. Be sure to invite someone who has reflected thoughtfully about being a member of that group in the United States and is willing to share his or her experiences.
- Discuss and evaluate the multicultural literature you read. Each group member needs to discuss and evaluate at least one book during the workshop and provide classmates with written reviews of all books read. Oral and written book reviews are to include (a) a brief summary of the text and illustrations; (b) an explanation of how the literary elements—characters, setting, plot, narrative style, and tone—are reflective of the nondominant culture; (c) a discussion of perspectives, values, attitudes, and points of view in the book that provide insight into the culture; and (d) concrete examples from the books to demonstrate the point made in (a) through (c). (Sometimes groups decide to read one book together and read other books separately. Sometimes all group members read different books.)
- Develop a description of the culture that emerges from a book and compare that image to the research findings.
- Identify common stereotypes and their origins.

- Share information pertaining to the cultural, social, religious, and economic aspects of the nondominant culture, which provide a background for understanding the literature reflecting that group.
- Share other things you found about the culture that you think are important for readers to know, and explain why.

All this works easier if the multicultural literature deals directly with discrimination, as did the literature read by Ann's students, but the process is applicable to all literature. Sometimes students won't find any cultural markers in the stories. Often this is because they have not developed their perception to a point that they can recognize them. Other times, students may become so sensitive to stereotypes and misrepresentations that they see things in the literature that are not there. However, they know that they must be able to support their assertions to the rest of the class. Although some questions may not have immediate resolutions, the discussion encourages students to recognize multiple perspectives and to continue searching for information that will contribute to understanding.

The most important part of a workshop experience may be listening to speakers from the nondominant cultures reflected in the literature who visit the class to talk about their life experiences. I think it is more effective if members of the groups invite the speakers and explain what they hope to learn from the speakers. But, the teacher may need to help. Sometimes parents can suggest people they know who may be willing to share. Individuals, families, or panels can provide interesting insights. If speakers can be present for the entire workshop, they are often willing to offer comments or to respond to any discussion. When speakers from nondominant cultures talk, my students listen very carefully. Students are honest and forthright and almost always tactful—they want to know. By the time a workshop is conducted, many students have been forced to confront their inability to imagine what it is like to be in a nondominant culture in the United States today, and they desperately want to know what it is like. I have found such face-to-face interactions irreplaceable.

Concluding the Story

Ann is a second-year teacher but she is already involved in a lifelong journey. She was satisfied, even happy, with some outcomes of this unit, but very unhappy about others. Like all good teachers, she already has begun to plan for next year. Ann's thinking has gone beyond the transformation stage. In this unit, she provided students with "the opportunity to formulate and justify their own versions of events and situations" (Banks, 2002, p. 31) by responding to literature. She taught them "to think critically and to develop the skills to formulate, document, and justify their conclusions and generalizations" (Banks, 2002, p. 31). By doing so, she has "acted personally and collectively on [her] learning" (Banks, 2002, p. 31). As she continues to do so, she will find new ways to bring students to the point of social action, also. Next time, the unit will be better, or maybe she will incorporate multicultural dimensions throughout the curriculum.

Theorists such as Banks (2002) and Nieto (2002) insist that not only must individual teachers change, but schools and systems must change. They talk about total societal reform. Ann, and teachers like her, are the backbone of that reform. When students and teachers change, schools change. Rosenblatt (1938/1976) writes,

> The development of literary appreciation will depend upon a reciprocal process: An enlargement of the student's understanding of human life leads to increased esthetic sensitivity, and increased esthetic sensitivity makes possible more fruitful human insights from literature. Efforts to heighten the student's appreciation of the formal qualities of the literary work will be organically related to the effort to enrich his sense of human values. (p. 273)

Multicultural literature is an aspect of multicultural education. If teachers take readers beyond identification with characters, beyond re-creating characters in their own images, to better understanding people who seem "other," they are helping to create a society in which people respect one another and, out of respect, listen on one another. That is what we are teaching—not listening in a literal sense, but listening in a profound sense. We are teaching readers to hear "the voice coming from the heart" (Cai, 1992, p. 26).

By telling the story of Ann's students and their experience with multicultural literature, I have tried to add voices of "real readers engaged with real texts in real contexts" (Cox, 1992, p. 20) to the dialogue currently under way. The voices of 123 dominant-culture readers participated in the telling of this story and, in one way or another, they all contributed to it. These students were fortunate to have a teacher who cared about them, loves literature, and who is committed to making the world a better one. The message that emerges from this story is bittersweet. Dominant-culture readers seldom recognize the unearned advantage they have merely by virtue of their color. Instead, they prefer to think that everyone has the same advantages. If we wish to help dominant-culture readers value others and celebrate diversity as natural and necessary, we need to help them recognize that their unearned advantage carries with it both the responsibility and the obligation to hear "the silent words on the pages [of multicultural literature]" (Cai, 1992, p. 26) and to respond with integrity to those voices.

> *It is what we think the world is like, not what it is really like, that determines our behavior. We act according to the way the world appears to us, not necessarily according to the way it is. (Boulding, as cited in Kegley & Wittkopf, 1989, p. 9)*

Book Club Organizer

Name_____ Period_____

DIRECTIONS: This packet is designed to help your Book Club keep track of its novel by providing a place for you to jot down different information about the novel.

Name of the novel: _____

Author of the novel: _____

Book Club members:_____   _____

_____   _____

_____   _____

Setting: Describe the setting(s) of the novel, including cultural specifics.

Point of View: Tell what point of view the author has chosen, define that point of view, and give several reasons why the author might have chosen that narrator.

Plot Line: Write one to three sentences telling what happened in each chapter. Be sure to include the most important events.

1.

2.

3.

4.

5.

6.

7.

8.

9.

10.

11.

12.

13.

14.

15.

16.

17.

Character List: As you read, note words/phrases/etc. that tell about each character.

1.	2.	3.
4.	5.	6.
7.	8.	9.
10.	11.	12.

Conflict: Think about the problems the characters face and how they handle these problems.

Dilemma Facing Character	Decision/Choice of Character	Reasons Character Made That Decision/Choice

What kinds of conflict did the characters face?

What forces created these conflicts?

Culture: What did you learn about the world your characters live in? What is valued in their world? What do they believe in? How does it compare and/or contrast with the world you live in?

Observation	Value/Belief	Comparison/Contrast

What stereotypes of this culture are promoted by the novel?

What stereotypes of this culture are destroyed by the novel?

Is this novel an authentic representation of this culture? Why or why not?

Symbols: What images/symbols come up repeatedly in the novel? Fill in the chart below:

Image/Object	Situations in Which It Occurs	Possible Significance

What does each symbol mean in the story?

Theme: What are some main points the author is telling us about life, people, or the world through this novel?

Dialogue Journal

Name_____   Period_____

Partner_____

DIRECTIONS: During the book club unit, you are required to keep a Dialogue Journal. This will help you clarify your thinking about the novel and communicate what you have learned to someone else. Partners will learn to read more insightfully and ask questions that make people think about what they have said. *The journal will take the form of letters. Each letter will be worth 10 points.* Date each of your letters. **Roles and responsibilities for each person are as follows:**

1. **Journaler:** You will *select a character* from the book and write about the story, events, yourself, and other characters *from his/her point of view*. Sometimes I will give you a specific topic to address in your letter, and sometimes you will write about what you are most concerned with. You should remain true to the point of view of the character you have selected. Your letter will be addressed to the responder and signed by the character.

2. **Responder:** You will read what the journaler has written very carefully and *respond in a careful and thoughtful manner*. You should (a) point out inconsistencies in what the character says; (b) ask for explanations of things that you do not understand; and (c) encourage the character to be more specific about what he/she means. You should take seriously everything that the character writes, but question everything so that both of you learn more. Your letter will be addressed to the character and signed by you.

Write as much as you can (and make sure it can be read, please). Enjoy!

Pre-Unit Survey

Name_____   Period_____   Date_____

DIRECTIONS: Fill out this information sheet *as completely as possible*. You will be graded on completeness and honesty. **Nothing you say will be counted against you** as long as you are being honest and use appropriate language.

1. How do you usually feel about reading a new novel? Why?

_____

_____

_____

_____

2. How do you usually feel about reading a novel whose characters have a different background and history from yours? Why?

_____

_____

_____

_____

3. a) What positive things do you know/believe about people from South Africa?

_____

_____

_____

_____

   b) Where did you learn that?

_____

_____

_____

_____

c) What negative things do you know/believe about people from South Africa?

_____

_____

_____

_____

d) Where did you learn that?

_____

_____

_____

_____

e) How do you know all of this information is accurate?

_____

_____

_____

_____

4. a) What positive things do you know/believe about people from Pakistan?

_____

_____

_____

_____

b) Where did you learn that?

_____

_____

_____

_____

c) What negative things do you know/believe about people from Pakistan?

_____

_____

_____

_____

d) Where did you learn that?

_____

_____

_____

_____

e) How do you know all of this information is accurate?

_____

_____

_____

_____

5. a) What positive things do you know/believe about people who are Chinese American?

_____

_____

_____

_____

b) Where did you learn that?

_____

_____

_____

_____

c) What negative things do you know/believe about people who are Chinese American?

_____

_____

_____

_____

d) Where did you learn that?

_____

_____

_____

_____

e) How do you know all of this information is accurate?

_____

_____

_____

_____

6. a) What positive things do you know/believe about people who are African American?

_____

_____

_____

_____

b) Where did you learn that?

_____

_____

_____

_____

c) What negative things do you know/believe about people who are African American?

_____

_____

_____

_____

d) Where did you learn that?

_____

_____

_____

_____

e) How do you know all of this information is accurate?

_____

_____

_____

_____

7. a) What positive things do you know/believe about people who are Latino American?

_____

_____

_____

_____

b) Where did you learn that?

_____

_____

_____

_____

c) What negative things do you know/believe about people who are Latino American?

_____

_____

_____

_____

d) Where did you learn that?

_____

_____

_____

_____

e) How do you know all of this information is accurate?

_____

_____

_____

_____

8. a) What positive things do you know/believe about people who are Vietnamese American?

_____

_____

_____

_____

b) Where did you learn that?

_____

_____

_____

_____

c) What negative things do you know/believe about people who are Vietnamese American?

_____

_____

_____

_____

d) Where did you learn that?

_____

_____

_____

_____

e) How do you know all of this information is accurate?

_____

_____

_____

_____

9. Define the word "culture" to the best of your ability and understanding:

_____

_____

_____

_____

10. Name as many unique characteristics of your culture as you can:

_____

_____

_____

_____

Post-Unit Survey

Name_____ Period_____ Date_____

DIRECTIONS: Fill out this information sheet *as completely as possible*. You will be graded on completeness and honesty. **Nothing you say will be counted against you** as long as you are being honest and use appropriate language.

1. How did you feel about reading this novel? Why?

_____

_____

_____

_____

2. Would you choose to read another novel whose characters have a different background and history from yours in the future? Why or why not?

_____

_____

_____

_____

3. a) What positive things do you know/believe about people from South Africa?

_____

_____

_____

_____

b) Where did you learn that?

_____

_____

_____

_____

c) What negative things do you know/believe about people from South Africa?

_____

_____

_____

_____

d) Where did you learn that?

_____

_____

_____

_____

e) How do you know all of this information is accurate?

_____

_____

_____

_____

4. a) What positive things do you know/believe about people from Pakistan?

_____

_____

_____

_____

b) Where did you learn that?

_____

_____

_____

_____

c) What negative things do you know/believe about people from Pakistan?

_____

_____

_____

_____

d) Where did you learn that?

_____

_____

_____

_____

e) How do you know all of this information is accurate?

_____

_____

_____

_____

5. a) What positive things do you know/believe about people who are Chinese American?

_____

_____

_____

_____

b) Where did you learn that?

_____

_____

_____

_____

c) What negative things do you know/believe about people who are Chinese American?

_____

_____

_____

_____

d) Where did you learn that?

_____

_____

_____

_____

e) How do you know all of this information is accurate?

_____

_____

_____

_____

6. a) What positive things do you know/believe about people who are African American?

_____

_____

_____

_____

b) Where did you learn that?

_____

_____

_____

_____

c) What negative things do you know/believe about people who are African American?

_____

_____

_____

_____

d) Where did you learn that?

_____

_____

_____

_____

e) How do you know all of this information is accurate?

_____

_____

_____

_____

7. a) What positive things do you know/believe about people who are Latino American?

_____

_____

_____

_____

b) Where did you learn that?

_____

_____

_____

_____

c) What negative things do you know/believe about people who are Latino American?

_____

_____

_____

_____

d) Where did you learn that?

_____

_____

_____

_____

e) How do you know all of this information is accurate?

_____

_____

_____

_____

8. a) What positive things do you know/believe about people who are Vietnamese American?

_____

_____

_____

_____

b) Where did you learn that?

_____

_____

_____

_____

c) What negative things do you know/believe about people who are Vietnamese American?

_____

_____

_____

_____

d) Where did you learn that?

_____

_____

_____

_____

e) How do you know all of this information is accurate?

_____

_____

_____

_____

9. a) What positive things do you know/believe about people who are Korean American?

_____

_____

_____

_____

b) Where did you learn that?

_____

_____

_____

_____

c) What negative things do you know/believe about people who are Korean American?

_____

_____

_____

_____

d) Where did you learn that?

_____

_____

_____

_____

e) How do you know all of this information is accurate?

_____

_____

_____

_____

10. Define the word "culture" to the best of your ability and understanding:

_____

_____

_____

_____

11. Name as many unique characteristics of your culture as you can:

_____

_____

_____

_____

Evaluation Instrument

Rater # _____   Student # _____

PLEASE ANSWER THE FOLLOWING QUESTIONS USING THE MATERIALS
IDENTIFIED:

1. Which book did the student read?
   (a) *Scorpions*   (e) *Shabanu: Daughter of the Wind*
   (b) *Journey of the Sparrows*   (f) *Waiting for the Rain*
   (c) *Shadow of the Dragon*   (g) *Morning Girl*
   (d) *Finding My Voice*

2. Which assignments are available for this student?
   (a) Pre-Unit Survey about novels read   (d) Dialogue Journal—Journaler
   (b) Post-Unit Survey about novels read (e) Dialogue Journal—Responder
   (c) Book Club Organizer

3. The reader is   (a) female   (b) male

PLEASE ANSWER THE FOLLOWING QUESTIONS ABOUT THE PRE-UNIT SURVEY:

4. The answer to Question 1 (How do you usually feel about reading a new novel? Why?) was
   (a) positive   (e) no paper
   (b) negative   (f) other
   (c) neutral
   (d) doesn't like reading/has trouble reading/doesn't like assignment
       (circle one or add another)

5. The answer to Question 2 (How do you usually feel about reading a novel whose characters have a different background and history from yours? Why?) was
   (a) positive   (e) no paper
   (b) negative   (f) other
   (c) neutral
   (d) doesn't like reading/has trouble reading/doesn't like assignment
       (circle one or add another)

PLEASE ANSWER THE FOLLOWING QUESTIONS ABOUT THE POST-UNIT SURVEY:

6. The answer to Question 1 (How did you feel about reading this novel? Why?) was
   - (a) positive
   - (b) negative
   - (c) neutral
   - (d) doesn't like reading/has trouble reading/doesn't like assignment
   - (e) no paper
   - (f) other
        (circle one or add another)

7. The answer to Question 2 (Would you choose to read another novel whose characters have a different background and history from yours in the future? Why or why not?) was
   - (a) positive
   - (b) negative
   - (c) neutral
   - (d) doesn't like reading/has trouble reading/doesn't like assignment
   - (e) no paper
   - (f) other
        (circle one or add another)

PLEASE ANSWER THE FOLLOWING QUESTIONS ABOUT THE BOOK CLUB ORGANIZER:

8. Is there evidence to indicate that the reader did not enjoy reading the book?
   - (a) yes
   - (b) no
   - (c) not possible to tell
   - (d) no paper

9. Is there evidence that the reader recognizes that the primary character(s) from the non-dominant culture operates (makes decisions, acts, and reacts) using a different set of underlying cultural assumptions/values/beliefs/loyalties from those of the dominant culture?
   - (a) appears to recognize this
   - (b) does not appear to recognize this
   - (c) not possible to tell
   - (d) no paper

10. The reader sees the character(s) from the non–European culture primarily
    - (a) as having the same freedom to act as the reader
    - (b) from a paternalistic point of view
    - (c) as "the other"—them, gang member, immigrant, blacks
    - (d) as having a dual identity
    - (e) not possible to tell
    - (f) no paper

11. Except in places calling for generalization, does the reader generalize from the non–European characters in the story to all members of that group?
    - (a) yes
    - (b) no
    - (c) not possible to tell
    - (d) no paper

12. Did the reader challenge or question the reflection of the nondominant cultural group or any aspects of it in the novel read?
    - (a) yes
    - (b) no
    - (c) not possible to tell
    - (d) no paper

13. Conscious or unconscious learning about the nondominant culture reflected in the book tends
    (a) toward a realistic understanding   (c) not possible to tell
    (b) to be primarily stereotypical   (d) no paper

14. Does the reader give evidence of conscious recognition of the norms and values of cultures different from the dominant culture?
    (a) yes   (b) no   (c) not possible to tell   (d) no paper

15. Does the reader give evidence of an increased understanding of himself or herself, his or her cultural values, or his or her cultural norms more clearly?
    (a) yes   (b) no   (c) not possible to tell   (d) no paper

16. This reader consciously or unconsciously notes obvious aspects of the nondominant culture such as food or skin color.
    (a) yes   (b) no   (c) not possible to tell   (d) no paper

17. This reader consciously or unconsciously recognizes characteristics of the nondominant culture such as family patterns and responsibilities, age and gender roles, preservation of honor, or impact of religion
    (a) as aspects of culture
    (b) not as aspects of culture but as idiosyncrasies of individual people/families
    (c) does not recognize them at all
    (d) not possible to tell
    (e) no paper

18. On page 5 of the Book Club Organizer,
    (a) the reader identifies stereotypes "promoted" in the book
    (b) the reader does not identify stereotypes "promoted" in the book
    (c) the reader does not appear to understand the meaning of *stereotype*
    (d) it is not possible to tell if the reader understands the meaning of *stereotype*
    (e) no paper

19. On page 5 of the Book Club Organizer,
    (a) the reader identifies stereotypes "destroyed" in the book
    (b) the reader does not identify stereotypes "destroyed" in the book
    (c) the reader does not appear to understand the meaning of *stereotype*
    (d) it is not possible to tell if the reader understands the meaning of *stereotype*
    (e) no paper

PLEASE ANSWER THE FOLLOWING QUESTION ABOUT THE DIALOGUE JOURNAL:

20. Is it clear that the reader is operating within the story world?
    (a) yes   (b) no   (c) can't tell for sure   (d) no paper

21. Does the reader internalize, implicitly or explicitly, the impact ethnicity has on the life of the character(s) of the nondominant culture?
    (a) yes   (b) no   (c) can't tell for sure   (d) no paper

22. Does the reader
    (a) assume the role of the character revealing the character's struggles/motivations/actions resulting from being of a nondominant culture?
    (b) assume the role of the character without revealing the character's struggles/motivations/actions resulting from being of a nondominant culture?
    (c) assume the role of the character, but appear to respond more as the reader (than the character) would have in the story situation?
    (d) assume the role of the dominant-culture character?
    (e) no paper

23. Is there evidence to indicate that the reader did not enjoy reading the book?
    (a) yes   (b) no   (c) not possible to tell   (d) no paper

24. Is there evidence that the reader recognizes that the primary character(s) from the non-dominant culture operates (makes decisions, acts, reacts) using a different set of underlying cultural assumptions, values, beliefs, or loyalties from those of the dominant culture?
    (a) appears to recognize this   (c) not possible to tell
    (b) does not appear to recognize this   (d) no paper

25. The reader sees the character(s) from the non–European culture primarily
    (a) as having the same freedom to act as the reader
    (b) from a paternalistic point of view
    (c) as "the other"—them, gang member, immigrant, blacks
    (d) as having a dual identity
    (e) not possible to tell
    (f) no paper

26. Except in places calling for generalization, does the reader generalize from the non-European characters in the story to all members of that group?
    (a) yes   (b) no   (c) not possible to tell   (d) no paper

27. Did the reader challenge or question the reflection of the nondominant cultural group or any aspects of it in the novel read?
    (a) yes   (b) no   (c) not possible to tell   (d) no paper

28. Conscious or unconscious learning about the nondominant culture reflected in the book tends
    (a) toward a realistic understanding   (c) not possible to tell
    (b) to be primarily stereotypical   (d) no paper

29. Does the reader give evidence of conscious recognition of the norms and values of a culture different from the dominant culture?
    (a) yes   (b) no   (c) not possible to tell   (d) no paper

30. Does the reader give evidence of an increased understanding of himself or herself, his or her cultural values, or his or her cultural norms?
    (a) yes   (b) no   (c) not possible to tell   (d) no paper

31. This reader consciously or unconsciously notes obvious aspects of the nondominant culture such as food or skin color.
    (a) yes   (b) no   (c) not possible to tell   (d) no paper

32. This reader consciously or unconsciously recognizes characteristics of the nondominant culture such as family patterns and responsibilities, age and gender roles, preservation of honor, or impact of religion
    (a) as aspects of culture
    (b) not as aspects of culture, but as idiosyncrasies of individual people/families
    (c) the reader does not recognize them at all
    (d) not possible to tell
    (e) no paper

PLEASE ANSWER THE FOLLOWING QUESTIONS ABOUT THE POST-UNIT SURVEY:

33. Does the reader identify books read for this unit as a source of learning?
    (a) yes   (b) no   (c) not possible to tell   (d) no paper

34. The student's responses on the Post-Unit Survey appear
    (a) to accurately reflect the nondominant culture
    (b) to be positive but stereotypical
    (c) to be negative but stereotypical
    (d) to be paternalistic and stereotypical
    (e) to reflect a neutral attitude
    (f) can't tell
    (g) no paper
    (h) other

35. The student's responses on the Post-Unit Survey are different from responses on the Pre-Unit Survey in that
    (a) they appear to more accurately reflect the nondominant culture
    (b) they appear to be more positive although they may still be stereotypical
    (c) they are still stereotypical but appear to be more negative
    (d) there appears to be little if any change
    (e) can't tell
    (f) no paper
    (g) other

36. Is there evidence to indicate that the reader did not enjoy reading the book?
    (a) yes   (b) no   (c) not possible to tell   (d) no paper

37. Is there evidence that the reader recognizes that the primary character(s) from the non-dominant culture operates (makes decisions, acts, reacts) using a different set of under-lying cultural assumptions, values, beliefs, or loyalties from those of the dominant culture?
    (a) appears to recognize this   (c) not possible to tell
    (b) does not appear to recognize this   (d) no paper

38. The reader sees the character(s) from the non–European culture primarily
    (a) as having the same freedom to act as the reader
    (b) from a paternalistic point of view
    (c) as "the other"—them, gang member, immigrant, blacks
    (d) as having a dual identity
    (e) not possible to tell
    (f) no paper

39. Does the reader acknowledge variation within the cultural group reflected in the novel?
    (a) yes   (d) no paper
    (b) no   (e) other
    (c) not possible to tell

40. From the Pre- to the Post-Unit Survey, the student's conscious or unconscious learning about the nondominant culture reflected in the books read appears to have become
    (a) more realistic   (d) no paper
    (b) more stereotypical   (e) no change
    (c) not possible to tell

41. Does the reader give evidence of conscious recognition of the norms and values of a culture different from the dominant culture?
    (a) yes   (b) no   (c) not possible to tell   (d) no paper

42. Does the reader give evidence of an increased understanding of himself/herself, his/her cultural values, or his/her cultural norms more clearly?

(a) yes   (b) no   (c) not possible to tell   (d) no paper

43. This reader consciously or unconsciously notes obvious aspects of the nondominant culture such as food or skin color:

(a) yes   (b) no   (c) not possible to tell   (d) no paper

44. This reader consciously or unconsciously recognizes characteristics of the nondominant culture such as family patterns and responsibilities, age and gender roles, preservation of honor, or impact of religion

(a) as aspects of culture

(b) not as aspects of culture but as idiosyncrasies of individual people/families

(c) does not recognize them at all

(d) not possible to tell

(e) no paper

45. On the Pre- and Post-Unit Surveys, where do students learn about people of cultures different from theirs?

(a) books read in this class

(b) books

(c) news

(d) school

(e) commercials

(f) magazines

(g) common knowledge

(h) "I just know"

(i) personal experience

(j) parents

(k) don't know

(l) movies

(m) people

(n) family/home

(o) television

(p) newspapers

(q) teachers

(r) no paper

(s) other:_____

PLEASE CONSIDER ALL ASSIGNMENTS WHEN ANSWERING THE FOLLOWING QUESTIONS:

46. Does the reader appear to recognize that *Korean American* and *Korean* are different, that *African American* and *African* are different, etc.?

(a) yes   (b) no   (c) can't tell   (d) no paper

47. Does the reader equate *South African* or *African* with *African American*?

(a) yes   (b) no   (c) can't tell   (d) no paper

Student's grade: _____

CTBS score: _____

Rubric for Training Raters

General Instructions

- The same questions are often asked of more than one assignment. When several numbers appear before a paragraph, the subsequent discussion refers to all the questions. Because not all options need clarification (for example, "no paper"), some are not included in this rubric.

- The term *nondominant* in the context of the Evaluation Instrument means *other* than European or white, or in *Shabanu*, not male. The nondominant cultures represented in the novels read are as follows:

Scorpions	African American/Hispanic
Journey of the Sparrows	Hispanic American/Hispanic
Shadow of the Dragon	Vietnamese American/Vietnamese
Finding My Voice	Korean American/Korean
Shabanu: Daughter of the Wind	Female
Waiting for the Rain	Black South African
Morning Girl	Native American/Taino

- Select "can't tell" only if it is not possible to decide given the information available. For example, mark "can't tell" if

  - the reader is so neutral, no decision can be made from what is written;
  - there is evidence to support either a "yes" or "no" answer, but you cannot determine from the writing which is meant;
  - the reader has not completed this section of the assignment, so it is not possible to make a decision.

Rubric for Specific Questions

Questions 4–7 determine

(a) whether the reader liked the multicultural book read,

(b) whether the reader felt positively enough about the book to read another multicultural book, or

(c) whether the reader's attitude about reading multicultural books changes from the Pre- to the Post-Unit Survey.

Even when the responder does not respond directly to the questions, try to determine if the answer is positive or negative. To be consistent, use the following definitions:

- Neutral = indication that the reader feels "it's OK" or "I don't mind," as opposed to feeling positive or negative.
- Positive = any indication that the reader feels more positive than neutral.
- Negative = any indication that the reader feels more negative than neutral.

Questions 8, 23, and 36 ask of the Book Club Organizer, the Dialogue Journal, and the Post-Unit Survey, respectively, whether the reader did or did not enjoy reading the book. The goal is to be sure that the answer to questions 6 and 7 are verified by the reader throughout the reading experience.

Questions 9, 24, and 37 assume that a different worldview is recognized if the reader recognizes one or more of the following:

- that a character's actions evolve from a unique set of assumptions, values, beliefs, and loyalties—often different from the values and beliefs of the reader—that are shared by members of the culture;
- that even though the actions of a character with a different worldview seem similar to the actions the reader might take, the reasons for those actions are often different;
- that people of a culture share a common way of seeing the world.

For example, in *Shadow of the Dragon*, the main character rescues two girls from aggressive members of a gang. A reader from the dominant culture might see this way of acting as brave or heroic while a member of the culture reflected in the book may see it simply as his duty because the main character is male.

The reader does not need to demonstrate what the different worldview is, only to recognize that there is one. A worldview is characteristic of a culture, not the direct result of a situation such as war (although such situations may affect worldview over time).

Questions 10, 25, and 38 ask if the reader sees the character(s) from the non–European culture primarily

(a) as having the same freedom to act as the reader

Choose this if the reader reacts to nondominant-culture characters in the same way he or she is likely to react to dominant-culture characters by assuming that the character from the nondominant culture has the same freedom to act as a dominant-culture character would. For example, the reader does not recognize constraints on blacks, Vietnamese, or Hispanics when those constraints are a result of their cultural affiliation. If the reader recognizes that the character's life is not like his or hers, that recognition must make a difference in how the reader portrays the attitude or assurance with which the character acts. Therefore, the reader who says Tengo "decides" to go to school, as if he were free to do whatever he chose, assumes that Tengo has the freedom to act. The assumption results in stereotypical learning and permits the reader to conclude, for example, that the life of a slave is not really so bad.

(b) from a paternalistic point of view

Paternalistic involves responses such as being altruistic, defending the group, or explaining the group (for example, "not all blacks are in gangs," "racism harms everyone," "immigration is tough").

(c) as "the other" (for example, "them," gang member, immigrant, black)

This way of thinking about nondominant characters sets them apart. Assuming characters are "other" is more "exclusive" and assumes an us-versus-them attitude. It often appears as a label. It may be derogatory. It always assumes the nondominant character is different or set apart from the reader and the cultural group with which that reader identifies. It is often closely related to the "problem" behavior in the story, which the reader perceives as characteristic of the cultural group.

(d) as having a dual identity

The reader recognizes the character's situation of living between two cultures—of living with a dual identity. The reader recognizes that because the character's culture "shows," the character is always a "qualified" person—an African American, a Korean American, a black South African, a female Pakistani. As a result, the character has to act accordingly and does not have the same freedom to act as the reader or another dominant-culture person does in (a) above.

(e) not possible to tell

The reader describes things so matter-of-factly that it is impossible to determine how the reader perceives the characters.

Questions 11 and 26: Does the reader generalize from the non–European characters in the story to all members of that group?

The reader may make blanket statements about the group when that is called for (for example, on page 5 of the Book Club Organizer: What did you learn about the world your characters live in? What do they believe in?), but to generalize from the character to the group is to make specific connections that all members of that group do things because the story character did. The key here is to decide whether the reader is commenting on a specific book or using the specific book as a representation of the whole group. So, for example, "There was gangs" is a comment on the specific story, but "Vietnamese people join gangs" is probably a generalization; "People traveled in crates to Mexico" is a comment on the specific story; "Whites had it better than blacks" is also a comment about a specific story when made in relation to *Waiting for the Rain*. When the reader goes beyond characters to the group in general in the real or story world, answer "yes."

Questions 12 and 27: Merely identifying something as a stereotype is not sufficient to say the reader is challenging the reflection of the group, although the manner of identifying the stereotype *may* indicate that the reader is doing so. For example, recognizing that "there are a lot of stereotypes put on blacks" in a specific book is to challenge the way the author portrays the group.

Questions 13 and 28: Conscious or unconscious learning about the nondominant culture reflected in the book

    (a) tends toward a realistic understanding

        This means *realistic* given the book read. Realistic involves respect and might be reflected in a reader's identifying with the nondominant-culture character as an equal and accepting the character's life as "normal," or in the reader's recognition that, for example, "Asian attitudes" as a stereotype are dispelled in the novel, or in the reader's recognition that Asian or Asian American characters "believing in spirits" is "different" rather than "bad," indicating that the reader has an understanding of the group that could be described as tending toward realistic. It could also mean recognizing inequality that exists, for example, in the "friendship" of Frikke and Tengo in *Waiting for the Rain*.

    (b) tends to be primarily stereotypical

        This might be reflected in an attitude that says that "American" is OK, but Vietnamese is old-fashioned and conservative. Sometimes the reader's learning appears to be realistic, but the reader reflects a pejorative attitude that denies differences or sees differences as negative.

(c) not possible to tell

The reader, for example, phrases all comments to reflect a realistic "this is the way things are" tone but the reader reads from a dominant-culture perspective. If, for example, in *Waiting for the Rain*, Frikke is seen as the main character, but Tengo is defined as *Frikke's good friend*, the reader does not recognize the power differential between whites and blacks in South Africa. As a result, the reader appears to accept blacks and does not reflect obvious or blatant stereotypes in his or her writing, but always *assumes* a power position.

Questions 14, 29, and 41: Does the reader give evidence of conscious recognition of the norms and values of a culture different than his or her own?

These need to be values appropriate to the specific culture. If a reader recognizes that Chinese Americans make decisions because of their valuing of Tet (the Chinese New Year), or if a reader writes that people of the culture reflected in the book read "practice religions different than ours; I think some of the religions are a little strange but that is probably because I'm only used to my religion," the readers recognize the norms and values of the respective cultures. Stereotypical values do not qualify, for example, identifying saving money to buy things as a Chinese American value. The reader needs to recognize consciously that the norms and values differ from his or hers but does not need to recognize that they are aspects of culture or how they translate into a specific worldview (as is necessary in #17). For example, recognizing male dominance in a culture does not mean that a reader will necessarily recognize it as it is played out in the lives of the characters.

Questions 15, 30, and 42: Giving evidence of increased understanding of self, cultural values, or cultural norms might be revealed by an explicit or implicit statement about the reader's own culture which reflects insight directly related to the story. This often appears on page 5 of the Book Club Organizer where readers are asked about culture. Some examples are

"We do not get married until about 20. I don't know why, but parents think we are too young and don't know anything" (comparing her life to that of Shabanu's).

"For some reason, African-Americans make me uncomfortable; I just don't know how to act or what to say when I'm around them."

Questions 16, 31, and 43: To refer, either directly or indirectly, to an obvious physical or surface characteristic (e.g., slanted eyes; kimchi; the chadar; tortillas; language; describing Chinese Americans as short and making good food; or perceiving all African Americans as good athletes) perceived as characteristic of particular cultures. Tet may be seen either as a "culture parade" type of holiday or may be recognized as an integral part of the culture. "There is racism" does not indicate conscious or unconscious recognition of obvious aspects of culture, but in the absence of evidence to the contrary, "a girl was Korean" and "a Korean girl" do indicate conscious or unconscious recognition of physical characteristics associated with a culture. Religion can be a label or can imply an impact on action. For example, "very religious family" implies an impact on action while "they were Catholic" is probably just a label.

Questions 17, 32, and 44 follow up Questions 16, 31, and 43 in an attempt to determine if the reader consciously or unconsciously recognized more sophisticated understandings of underlying cultural differences: responsibilities and interaction patterns within the family, either nuclear or extended; the effect of underlying beliefs about age and gender; preservation of honor; or impact of religious beliefs. Recognizing a characteristic as an aspect of culture means that it is not used merely as a stereotypical label.

(a) as aspects of culture

There must be some conscious recognition that aspects identified are related to the character's cultural affiliation. For example, in *Shadow of the Dragon* a reader might recognize that because of the characters' Vietnamese heritage, Danny skips a date to find his sister, Grandma is old-fashioned and strictly religious, Hong is old-fashioned with no use for American girls, or Kim wants to fit in with American girls.

(b) not as aspects of culture, but as idiosyncrasies of individual people/families

The reader gives no indication of conscious recognition that aspects identified are related to culture. For example, Danny just acts as he does in *Shadow of the Dragon*. While it may be because of his family, the reader does not indicate any awareness that this type of family interaction is likely to reflect Vietnamese culture.

Questions 18 and 19: Sometimes it is not possible to tell if readers understand the meaning of *stereotype*. It appears that readers are able to identify negative stereotypes, but, when asked for stereotypes promoted, they tend to offer a positive or realistic characteristic of the group, which counters their actual stereotype: "Some of these people are smart enough and care enough not to do bad things." As a result, it is not possible to determine for sure if such readers understand the meaning stereotype.

Question 21: *Ethnicity* here refers to "the basic divisions or groups of mankind, as distinguished by customs, characteristics, language" (*Webster's New World Dictionary*). Being part of a nondominant-culture group, at least within the United States, almost invariably results in an internal struggle as the person/character tries to live well in two worlds—the ethnically related world and the "American" world as defined by the dominant culture. The reader recognizes this struggle rather than perceiving the conflicts as external and imposing on the character(s). It is also important to distinguish between ethnicity and class or societal issues. For example, being in a gang is not a result of ethnicity, but the way a family reacts to a young person being in a gang may be. Or, in *Shadow of the Dragon*, Danny's need to be home for New Year's is directly related to his ethnicity, and to the values and norms he shares because he is part of a family with a Vietnamese heritage. Kids of other groups may need to be home, but the situation in *Shadow of the Dragon* is directly related to Danny's cultural background.

Question 22: Does the reader

(a) assume the role of the character revealing the character's struggles/motivations/ actions resulting from being of a nondominant culture?

If so, the reader "becomes" the character, intentionally (though not necessarily obviously or blatantly) revealing the character's connection with the culture.

(b) assume the role of the character *without* revealing the character's struggles/ motivations/actions resulting from being of a nondominant culture?

If so, the reader is likely to sound as though he or she is reporting.

(c) assume the role of the character, but appear to respond more as the reader (than the character) would have in the story situation?

If so, although using the character's name, the actions and responses are characteristic of the reader as evidenced in his or her writing, not of the character developed in the novel.

QUESTIONS 33–45 REFER TO THE POST-UNIT SURVEY ONLY UNLESS OTHERWISE SPECIFIED:

Question 33 asks for a simple identification: Does the reader say, anywhere, on the Post-Unit Survey that his or her information came from one of the books read in this unit? Identifying class presentations based on the novels indicates that the information is from one of the books.

Question 34: The Post-Unit Survey asks the reader to respond to questions about all cultures reflected in the novels the class read. Readers are asked what positive and negative things they know about people of a variety of cultures. Be alert to the fact that positives and negatives are different from stereotypes. For example, a reader who says that he or she "knows some African Americans, Hispanics, or Vietnamese are in gangs" is accurately reflecting information from the novels read in class. On the other hand, responses such as "African Americans are [all] poor" or "African Americans are [all] good in sports" are clearly stereotypical—the first almost always perceived as negative and the second as positive. Please consider any and all information included in the Post-Unit Survey when trying to determine whether the reader's responses appear to accurately reflect the nondominant culture. Are the reader's responses generally more accurate than stereotypical?

Question 35: The Pre- and Post-Unit Surveys ask readers to respond to questions about all cultures reflected in the novels the class read. Readers are asked what positive and negative things they know about people of a variety of cultures. Be alert to the fact that positives and negatives are different from stereotypes. Just because "we" do not like the answer does not make it less realistic. For example, a reader who says that he or she "knows some African Americans, Hispanics, or Vietnamese are in gangs" is accurately reflecting information from the novels read in class. On the other hand, a response such as "African Americans are [all] poor or good in sports" is clearly stereotypical, the first almost always perceived as negative and the second as positive. A more specific answer may appear to be negative but may be more realistic than naive platitudes. Please consider any and all information included in both surveys when trying to determine whether the reader's responses appear to have changed or not to have changed from the beginning to the end of the unit:

(a) responses appear to reflect the nondominant culture more accurately

There are many cultures about which readers must respond. Responses do not need to be realistic, but are they **more** realistic than on the Pre-Unit Survey? Sometimes this is a tough call, but, if the reader has gone from stereotypical (positive or negative) or naive statements to "I don't know much about...," recognizing what he or she doesn't know; or, if the reader assumes that Korean is Chinese American but the learning offsets earlier negative feelings about Chinese Americans, both responses can be considered as more accurately reflecting the nondominant culture.

(b) responses appear to be more positive although they may still be stereotypical

Although the responses appear to be stereotypical, they are more positive than on the reader's Pre-Unit Survey. For example, the reader may identify specifics that tend to be less negative, from "Pakistani's ate wild dogs in the 1900's" to "they can't choose who they are going to marry."

(c) responses still appear to be stereotypical but appear to be more negative

The responses appear to be stereotypical but are more negative than the reader's responses on the Pre-Unit Survey.

(d) there appears to be little if any change

There is little change in the nature or tenor of the reader's responses from the Pre-Unit Survey to the Post-Unit Survey.

Question 39: Is the tendency for the reader to respond to a book as "representative" of a cultural group, or does the reader recognize that some members may do things in a particular way but not others? Look for key words such as *some*, *the majority*, *a lot of them* to indicate that the reader is not assuming that all people of a culture are the same. If you find this distinction about even one group, answer "yes."

Question 40: Consider a student's conscious or unconscious learning about the non-dominant culture to be "more realistic" if you can substantiate it. Sometimes, if an answer is based on books or presentations, the answer may appear negative but be realistic. For example, "some Vietnamese hate Americans" may be realistic learning in light of the grandmother's attitude and actions in *Shadow of the Dragon*. Other examples are

- "Chinese Americans are discriminated against because of their culture and looks" (even though learned from the group that read a book about Korean Americans).
- "African Americans were slaves; now they are treated better but are still discriminated against."
- "Vietnamese Americans have come to America for freedom and new life but don't get that much of a better life here; some fall in with gangs to make money and some rob others."

Question 46 asks for information about the reader at the end of the unit. Information from the Book Club Organizer, the Dialogue Journal, and both the Pre- and Post-Unit Surveys may be used to answer this question.

The question is meant to determine whether readers recognize that African Americans, Asian Americans, Hispanic Americans, and Native Americans are U.S. citizens. It is also meant to determine whether readers recognize that U.S. citizens are not the "same" as foreign nationals living in the United States or as natives of foreign countries.

Assume that readers maintain learning from the Pre- to the Post-Unit Survey. If readers recognize on the Pre-Unit Survey that *Vietnamese* and *Vietnamese American* are different, it makes sense to assume that they still know that at the end of the unit. On the other hand, if readers do not recognize on the Pre-Unit Survey that *Vietnamese* and *Vietnamese American* are different but do appear to know that on the Post-Unit Survey, assume that they have learned the difference by at the end of the unit. Readers tended to use the terms interchangeably or as identifiers for characters. Unless the reader recognizes the *American* part of every group, it is unlikely that he or she recognizes that people who are citizens are not the same as foreign nationals. For example, if the reader consistently uses *Korean* and *Korean American* interchangeably, it can be assumed that she does not recognize that they are different.

If the reader says about *Chinese Americans* that "their people are very smart," meaning that this group is not "American," assume that the reader does not recognize that *Chinese Nationals* and *Chinese Americans* are different even if the reader uses the both terms. If readers appear to recognize that Africans refer to people living "in Africa" while African Americans live in the United States, and that Native Americans are indigenous to the United States, but do not recognize that these people are "American" in the same way as dominant culture people are, answer "no" to the question.

REFERENCES

Allport, G.W. (1958). *The nature of prejudice*. New York: Perseus. (Original work published 1954)

Altieri, J.L. (1996). Children's written responses to multicultural texts: A look at aesthetic involvement and the focuses of aesthetically complex responses. *Reading Research and Instruction, 35*, 237–248.

Applebee, A.N. (1978). *The child's concept of story*. Chicago: University of Chicago Press.

Applebee, A.N. (1990). *Literature instruction in American schools* (Report Series 1.4). Albany, NY: National Research Center on Literature Teaching and Learning.

Bakhtin, M. (1981). *The dialogic imagination*. Austin, TX: University of Texas Press.

Banks, J.A. (2002). *An introduction to multicultural education* (3rd ed.). Boston: Allyn & Bacon.

Beach, R. (1997). Students' resistance to engagement with multicultural literature. In T. Rogers & A.O. Soter (Eds.), *Reading across cultures: Teaching literature in a diverse society* (pp. 69–94). New York: Teachers College Press; Urbana, IL: National Council of Teachers of English.

Beach, R., & Freedman, K. (1992). Responding as a cultural act: Adolescents' responses to magazine ads and short stories. In J. Many & C. Cox (Eds.), *Reader stance and literary understanding: Exploring the theories, research, and practice* (pp. 162–188). Norwood, NJ: Ablex.

Bishop, R.S. (1992). Multicultural literature for children: Making informed choices. In V.J. Harris (Ed.), *Teaching multicultural literature in grades K–8* (pp. 37–53). Norwood, MA: Christopher-Gordon.

Bishop, R.S. (1997). Foreword. In T. Rogers & A.O. Soter (Eds.), *Reading across cultures: Teaching literature in a diverse society* (pp. vii–ix). New York: Teachers College Press; Urbana, IL: National Council of Teachers of English.

Bleich, D. (1975). *Reading and feelings: An introduction to subjective criticism*. Urbana, IL: National Council of Teachers of English.

Britton, J. (1970). *Language and learning*. London: Allen Lane/Penguin Press.

Cai, M. (1992). *Towards a multi-dimensional model for the study of reader reponse to multicultural literature*. Unpublished doctoral dissertation, Ohio State University, Columbus.

Cai, M. (1997). Reader-response theory and the politics of multicultural literature. In T. Rogers & A.O. Soter (Eds.), *Reading across cultures: Teaching literature in a diverse society* (pp. 199–212). New York: Teachers College Press; Urbana, IL: National Council of Teachers of English.

Cai, M. (1998). Multiple definitions of multicultural literature: Is the debate really just 'ivory tower' bickering? *The New Advocate, 11*, 311–324.

Commission for Racial Equality. (1988). *Learning in terror: A survey of racial harassment in schools and colleges*. London: Author.

Cox, C., & Many, J. (1992). Beyond choosing: Emergent categories of efferent and aesthetic stances. In J. Many & C. Cox (Eds.), *Reader stance and literary understanding: Exploring the theories, research, and practice* (pp. 103–126). Norwood, NJ: Ablex.

Cruz, G., Jordan, S., Melendez, J., Ostrowski, S., & Purves, A.C. (1997). *Beyond the culture tours: Studies in teaching and learning with culturally diverse texts*. Mahwah, NJ: Erlbaum.

Dasenbrock, R.W. (1992). Teaching multicultural literature. In J. Trimmer & T. Warnock (Eds.), *Understanding others: Cultural and cross-cultural studies and the teaching of literature* (pp. 35–46). Urbana, IL: National Council of Teachers of English.

Donelson, K.L., & Nilsen, A.P. (1989). *Literature for young adults*. Glenview, IL: Scott, Foresman.

Dyson, A.H. (1993). *Social worlds of children learning to write in an urban primary school*. New York: Teachers College Press.

Eisner, E. (1992). The misunderstood role of the arts in human development. *Phi Delta Kappan, 8*, 591–595.

Enciso, P.E. (1997). Negotiating the meaning of difference: Talking back to multicultural literature. In T. Rogers & A.O. Soter (Eds.), *Reading across cultures: Teaching literature in a diverse society* (pp. 13–41). New York: Teachers College Press; Urbana, IL: National Council of Teachers of English.

Fish, S. (1980). *Is there a text in this class? The authority of interpretive communities*. Cambridge, MA: Harvard University Press.

Galda, L. (1992). Evaluation as a spectator: Changes across time and genre. In J. Many & C. Cox (Eds.), *Reader stance and literary understanding: Exploring the theories, research, and practice* (pp. 127–132). Norwood, NJ: Ablex.

Graham, J.W. (1985). *The effects of reading ethnic literature on the attitudes of adolescents*. Unpublished doctoral dissertation, Georgia State University, Atlanta.

Griffin, J.H. (1961). *Black like me*. New York: The New American Library/Signet.

Hade, D.D. (1997). Reading multiculturally. In V.J. Harris (Ed.), *Using multiethnic literature in the K–8 classroom* (pp. 233–256). Norwood, MA: Christopher-Gordon.

Hall, S. (1985). *Anti-racism in practice: Stuart Hall examines the implications of using ACER materials* [Video]. London: Inner London Education Authority; Afro-Caribbean Education Resource Centre.

Harding, D.W. (1962). Psychological processes in the reading of fiction. *The British Journal of Aesthetics, 6*, 247–258.

Harris, V. (1994). No invitations required to share multicultural literature. *Journal of Children's Literature, 20*, 9–13.

Heath, S.B. (1983). *Ways with words: Language, life, and work in communities and classrooms*. New York: Cambridge University Press.

Holland, N.H. (1975). *Five readers reading*. New Haven, CT: Yale University Press.

Iser, W. (1974). *The implied reader*. Baltimore: Johns Hopkins University Press.

Iser, W. (1978). *The act of reading: A theory of aesthetic response*. Baltimore: Johns Hopkins University Press.

Jordan, S. (1997). Student responses to culturally diverse texts. In G. Cruz, S. Jordan, J. Melendez, S. Ostrowski, & A.C. Purves, *Beyond the culture tours: Studies in teaching and learning with culturally diverse texts* (pp. 9–34). Mahwah, NJ: Erlbaum.

Jordan, S., & Purves, A.C. (1993). *Issues in the responses of students to culturally diverse texts: A preliminary study*. Retrieved March 3, 1998, from http://cela.albany.edu/issrespon/purvjord.html

Kegley, C.W., Jr., & Wittkopf, E.R. (1989). *World politics: Trend and transformation* (3rd ed.). New York: St. Martin's Press.

Langer, J.A. (1994). Focus on research: A response-based approach to reading literature. *Language Arts, 71*, 203–211.

Lensmire, T.J. (1994). *When children write: Critical re-visions of the writing workshop*. New York: Teachers College Press.

Macphee, J.S. (1997). That's not fair! A white teacher reports on white first graders' responses to multicultural literature. *Language Arts, 47,* 33–39.

Many, J.E., & Wiseman, D.L. (1992). Analyzing versus experiencing: The effects of teaching approaches on students' responses. In J. Many & C. Cox (Eds.), *Reader stance and literary understanding: Exploring the theories, research, and practice* (pp. 250–276). Norwood, NJ: Ablex.

Martin, J.-P. (1980). *The effects of selected black literature on the attitudes of white adolescents toward blacks.* Unpublished doctoral dissertation, University of Connecticut, Storrs.

Mathis, J.B. (2001, Spring). Challenging engagements—Critical response: An interview with Kathy G. Short. *Journal of Children's Literature, 27,* 56–63.

Mauro, L.H. (1984). *Personal constructs and response to literature: Case studies of adolescents reading about death.* Unpublished doctoral dissertation, Rutgers State University of New Jersey, New Brunswick.

McIntosh, P. (1989, July/August). White privilege: Unpacking the invisible knapsack. *Peace and Freedom,* 10–12.

Naidoo, B. (1992). *Through whose eyes? Exploring racism: Reader, text, and context.* Chester, UK: Trentham Books.

National Center for Education Statistics. (1997). *America's teachers: Profile of a profession, 1993-94* (NCES 97-460). Robin R. Henke, Susan P. Choy, Xianglei Chen, Sonya Geis, Martha Naomi Alt, & Stephen P. Broughman, Project Officer. Washington, DC: U.S. Department of Education.

Nieto, S. (2002). *Language, culture, and teaching: Critical perspectives for a new century.* Mahwah, NJ: Erlbaum.

Ostrowski, S. (1997). Teaching multicultural literature. In G. Cruz, S. Jordan, J. Melendez, S. Ostrowski, & A.C. Purves, *Beyond the culture tours: Studies in teaching and learning with culturally diverse texts* (pp. 47–68). Mahwah, NJ: Erlbaum.

Phelan, P., Davidson, A.L., & Cao, H.T. (1992). Speaking up: Students' perspectives on school. *Phi Delta Kappan, 73,* 695–704.

Purves, A.C. (1993). Toward a reevaluation of reader response and school literature. *Language Arts, 70,* 348–361.

Purves, A.C. (1997). Introduction: The grand tour and other forays. In G. Jordan, S. Cruz, J. Melendez, S. Ostrowski, & A.C. Purves. *Beyond the culture tours: Studies in teaching and learning with culturally diverse texts* (pp. 1–8). Mahwah, NJ: Erlbaum.

Purves, A.C., & Beach, R. (1972). *Literature and the reader: Research in response to literature, reading interests, and the teaching of literature.* Urbana, IL: National Council of Teachers of English.

Purves, A.C., Foshay, A.W., & Hansson, G. (1973). *Literature education in ten countries.* Stockholm: Almquist and Wiksell.

Reynolds, R.E., Taylor, M.A., Steffensen, M.S., Shirey, L.L., & Anderson, R.C. (1982). Cultural schemata and reading comprehension. *Reading Research Quarterly, 3,* 353–366.

Rice, P. (1999, November). *It 'ain't' always so: Students' interpretations of multicultural stories with universal themes.* Paper presented at the annual meeting of the National Council of Teachers of English, Denver, CO.

Robinson, R. (2002). *The reckoning: What blacks owe to each other.* New York: Dutton.

Rogers, T. (1991). Students as literary critics: The interpretative experiences, beliefs, and processes of ninth-grade students. *Journal of Reading Behavior, 23,* 391–423.

Rogers, T., & Soter, A.O. (Eds.). (1997). *Reading across cultures: Teaching literature in a diverse society.* New York: Teachers College Press; Urbana, IL: National Council of Teachers of English.

Rosenblatt, L.M. (1976). *Literature as exploration* (3rd ed.). New York: Noble and Noble. (Original work published 1938)

Rosenblatt, L.M. (1978). *The reader, the text, the poem: The transactional theory of the literary work.* Carbondale, IL: Southern Illinois University Press.

Rosenblatt, L.M. (1985). Viewpoints: Transaction versus interaction (A terminological rescue operation). *Research in the Teaching of English, 19,* 96–107.

Sims [Bishop], R. (1982). *Shadow and substance: Afro-American experience in contemporary children's fiction.* Urbana, IL: National Council of Teachers of English.

Steffensen, M.S., Joag-Dev, C., & Anderson, R.C. (1979). A cross-cultural perspective on reading comprehension. *Reading Research Quarterly, 15,* 10–29.

Tobin, B.J. (1989). *The responses of early adolescent, white Australian readers to selected cross-cultural, folklore-based fantasy novels by Patricia Wrightson.* Unpublished doctoral dissertation, University of Georgia, Athens.

Trimmer, J., & Tilly, W. (Eds.). (1992). Understanding others: Cultural and cross-cultural studies and the teaching of literature. Urbana, IL: National Council of Teachers of English.

Van Dyke, J. (1997). *A group case study of student teachers' reactions to multicultural literature discussion group readings.* Unpublished doctoral dissertation, Claremont Graduate School and San Diego State University, California.

Walker-Dalhouse, D. (1992). Fostering multicultural awareness: Books for young children. *Reading Horizons, 33,* 47–54.

Wason-Ellam, L. (1997). "If only I was like Barbie." *Language Arts, 74,* 430–437.

Wilhelm, J.D. (1997). *"You gotta BE the book": Teaching engaged and reflective reading with adolescents.* New York: Teachers College Press; Urbana, IL: National Council of Teachers of English.

Wong, N. (1994). When I was growing up. In M.M. Gillan & J. Gillan (Eds.), *Unsettling America* (p. 55). New York: Penguin.

Young, T.A., Campbell, L.C., & Oda, L.K. (1995). Multicultural literature for children and young adults: A rationale and resources. *Reading Horizons, 35,* 375–393.

Zimet, S.G. (1976). *Print and prejudice.* London: Hodder & Stoughton.

Note: Page numbers followed by *f* indicate figures; those followed by *t* indicate tables.

C

D

DOMINANT CULTURE, 2; assumption of superiority of, 66–67; and character assumption, 64–65, 72–73; cultural markers of, 109; and perceptions of multicultural literature, 47–50, 56, 71–72; and rejection of unknown voices, 92; responsibility of, 3

DONELSON, K.L., 17

DORRIS, M., 20

DUAL IDENTITY: struggles with, recognition of, 67–68

DYSON, A.H., 94

E

EFFERENT READING, 9; and significance, 34

EISNER, E., 40

EMPATHY: limits of, 96

ENCISO, P.E., 94

EVALUATION INSTRUMENT, 146–152; development of, 30–32

EXPERT READERS, 40

F

FISH, S., 9

FOSHAY, A.W., 12

FREEDMAN, K., 56, 71–72, 95

G

GALDA, L., 10, 77

GARLAND, S., 10, 18

GENDER: and response patterns, 42–43

GORDON, S., 18

GRAHAM, J.W., 71

GRIFFIN, J.H., 70, 72

H

HADE, D., 46

HALL, S., 46

V

VALUES: recognition of, 68–69, 73, 77
VAN DYKE, J., 98–99

W

WALKER-DALHOUSE, D., 1
WASON-ELLAM, L., 49–50
WHITE PRIVILEGE, 3, 69–70, 89, 99. *See also* dominant culture
WILHELM, J.D., 40–41, 103–104
WISEMAN, D.L., 33
WITTKOPF, E.R., 123
WONG, N., 88
WORKSHOPS, 119–121
WORLDVIEW: defaults in, 76–78; and reader response, 69; recognition of, 58–60, 104–105
WRITTEN RESPONSES: analysis of, 5–6; on enjoyment of multicultural literature, 34–45; versus oral, 32

Y–Z

YOUNG, T.A., 1
YOUTH CULTURE: impact of, 71–72
ZIMET, S.G., 46, 69, 87

DATE DUE

Demco, Inc. 38-293